SUPERIORITY
CONCEIT
in BUDDHIST
TRADITIONS

SUPERIORITY CONCEIT *in* BUDDHIST TRADITIONS

A HISTORICAL PERSPECTIVE

Bhikkhu Anālayo

FOREWORD BY
Richard Gombrich

Wisdom Publications
199 Elm Street
Somerville, MA 02144 USA
wisdomexperience.org

Library of Congress Cataloging-in-Publication Data
Names: Anālayo, 1962– author.
Title: Superiority conceit in Buddhist traditions: a historical perspective /
    Bhikkhu Anālayo; foreword by Richard Gombrich.
Description: Somerville, MA, USA: Wisdom Publications, 2021. |
    Includes bibliographical references and index.
Identifiers: LCCN 2020020795 (print) | LCCN 2020020796 (ebook) |
    ISBN 9781614297192 (hardcover) | ISBN 9781614297338 (ebook)
Subjects: LCSH: Buddhism—Doctrines—Miscellanea. | Buddhist ethics. |
    Snobs and snobbishness.
Classification: LCC BQ4095 .A53 2021 (print) | LCC BQ4095 (ebook) |
    DDC 294.3/42—dc23
LC record available at https://lccn.loc.gov/2020020795
LC ebook record available at https://lccn.loc.gov/2020020796

ISBN 978-1-61429-719-2   ebook ISBN 978-1-61429-733-8

25 24 23 22 21
5 4 3 2 1

Cover design by Gopa & Ted 2. Cover photograph by Alexandra Makkonen. Interior design by James Skatges. Set in Diacritical Garamond Pro 11.25/14.9.

As an act of Dhammadāna, Bhikkhu Anālayo has waived royalty payments for this book.

Printed on acid-free paper that meets the guidelines for permanence and durability of the Production Guidelines for Book Longevity of the Council on Library Resources.

Printed in the United States of America.

Those who are skilled
declare that to be one's bondage:
what one depends on
to look down on another as inferior.
(*Suttanipāta* 798)

Contents

Acknowledgments

I AM INDEBTED to Chris Burke, Bhikkhunī Dhammadinnā, Richard Gombrich, Linda Grace, Bhikkhu U Jāgara, and Yuka Nakamura for commenting on a draft version of this study or part of it.

Foreword

Since Bhikkhu Anālayo has done me the honour of inviting me to write a foreword to this book, I have been given the opportunity to read through it before he sends it to the printers, and I feel extremely privileged, because it has taught me a lot.

Throughout the book, two themes are skilfully interwoven. In conformity with the title, there is a moral theme: conceit. Anālayo analyses and criticises, as befits an experienced monk, the attitudes of those who in any way have participated in a branch of the Buddhist tradition, from its founding to the present day, while claiming that in some respect their ideas and practices are superior to those of other Buddhists, and that this superiority should be acknowledged and respected.

Ethics can be considered the foundation of Buddhist practice and is thus the topic of many a Buddhist sermon; besides, Buddhism has much to say about taming the ego and practising unselfishness. Nevertheless, I believe that rarely does one come across a discussion focussed on the vice of arrogance, and yet more rarely one on the arrogance which some people display about their identity as a Buddhist. In that sense, this book is a courageous endeavour to fill a gap.

While pursuing his ethical argument, Anālayo fleshes out his subtitle by pursuing his scholarly vocation in such a way as to use material from Buddhist history to justify his criticisms on factual grounds and reveal an astonishing series of misconceptions promulgated by ignorance of what the texts can teach us. Thus anyone who studies this book is likely to feel, as I do, that it deserves to be widely read and understood throughout the Buddhist world.

Anālayo's skill as an exegete is shown on every page by his ability in organising his wide-ranging material. He deals with conceit and the ignorance on which it is built in four parts. Respectively, these deal with the arrogance of the male sex and its unjust treatment of women; the rise of the Mahāyāna and the distortions in its view of non-Mahāyāna Buddhism; the narrow-minded pomposity of the Theravādin claim to be the Buddhist tradition which has remained uniquely faithful to the Buddha's teaching; and the megalomanic spirit of Buddhist movements arising around us today which claim to understand what the Buddha experienced better than he could himself. He lays out this basic structure (better than I have) both in the introduction and in the conclusion—and I would suggest that readers may find it helpful to read the conclusion before the rest of the book, and again after finishing it.

Similarly, each of the four parts ends with a summary of the arguments it contains. This appears to me another feature of the book which I find extremely welcome. Without detracting from any of its other qualities, Anālayo has used the writing of this book as an opportunity to summarise many of his earlier discoveries, presenting his conclusions with rather less of the scholarly apparatus which readers not so familiar with the detail required in academic publications often find daunting, and sometimes therefore skip over. Both morally and academically, Anālayo is telling us things about Buddhism which are not just interesting and personally helpful but should have massive practical consequences.

I have room for just one example. In part I of the book he shows that the stories of how the Buddha was reluctant to found an Order of Nuns have been partly invented and often misinterpreted by misogynists, and how moreover there is no scriptural justification for the refusal in some Theravāda countries to re-establish that Order. He has already published these arguments in the *Journal of the Oxford Centre for Buddhist Studies*, but very few people read such journals, and it is reasonable to hope that this book will reach a far wider public. Perhaps one may even make so bold as to think that if some Buddhists who hold positions of power in those countries can learn what this book could teach them, something may be done to stem the appalling decline of true Buddhist compassion and psychological insight in those countries—and in the rest of the world today.

Richard Gombrich

Introduction

Probably all Buddhist traditions would agree in principle that superiority conceit is a detrimental mental condition and better overcome. Yet, the historical reality of various forms of Buddhism reflects recurrent manifestations of superiority conceit. These can take the form of gender discrimination or of dismissive attitudes toward other Buddhist traditions. In the present brief study, I survey four chief manifestations of such superiority conceit, examined from the viewpoint of their historical evolution and in relation to relevant early Buddhist teachings found in discourses in the four main Pāli *Nikāyas* and their parallels preserved by other Buddhist transmission lineages. My concern in what follows is not to keep identifying instances where conceit manifests, but rather to explore the network of conditions that appear to underpin the four forms of superiority conceit taken up for study. For this reason, after an initial identification of the type of superiority conceit under study, the main exploration in each chapter involves a survey of historical developments, compared with relevant teachings in the early discourses.

In the first chapter I take up the superiority conceit of males. This manifests in particular in the form of opposition to granting full ordination to women who wish to live the monastic life. Another relevant strand is the perceived impossibility for females to become advanced bodhisattvas. The path to Buddhahood, as distinct from the path to arahantship, continues to be of relevance in the second chapter, in which I explore the claim made in some Mahāyāna traditions to be superior to those who do not aspire to become Buddhas in the future. With the third chapter I turn to the Theravāda traditions, critically examining the assumption that the central doctrines of this tradition reflect without any change the original teachings of the historical Buddha. The claim to superiority over other Buddhist traditions can manifest also in Secular Buddhism, which I examine in the fourth and last chapter.

Some of the research summarized in the following pages is comparatively recent, leaving open the possibility that future studies might reveal perspectives that prompt a revision of certain details presented here. However, I am confident that the main points presented will stand the test of time.

Considerable parts of the present exploration build on more-detailed individual studies by myself. In order to make more widely available academic research by myself and others, I have tried to present matters in a succinct way, which inevitably involves a simplification of what in actual fact are rather complex processes and conditions. Although comparative study and translation of the early discourses extant in Chinese, Pāli, Sanskrit, and Tibetan is my main area of research, in this book I just refer to translations of the primary sources and selected secondary literature. I also dispense with annotation, employing instead in-line quotations to enable the interested reader to follow up by consulting translations of the relevant passages or else relevant studies that provide a more-fine-grained and in-depth analysis of what I present here only in a summary manner.

Although fairly short, this book presents several challenges. Not all of these are easily digested, and I anticipate that some of my readers will not feel comfortable with the material collected here and will experience at least parts of it as unwelcome and even enervating. I would like to apologize in advance if anything I say is felt as an affront. It is definitely not my intention to offend or be dismissive, but only to offer perspectives that might help to diminish conceit, even though the medicine might at times taste bitter. In challenging the four types of conceit listed above, I do so as someone himself involved in a continuous struggle with my own types of conceit. That is, I do not intend to set myself apart and, from the safe distance of the uninvolved observer, issue challenges for others. Instead, I speak as one who still has quite some work to do with various manifestations of my own conceit.

When confronted with the forms of conceit studied in this book, time and again I found that an understanding of the religious and historical conditions responsible for a particular situation was both sobering and liberating. Insight into the why and how of certain aspects of the Buddhist traditions can help to see these in the proper perspective and find ways to adjust. For this reason, I hope that the material presented here will be helpful to the reader, enabling a more informed perspective and consequently a letting go of ignorance and conceit.

I. Buddhist Androcentrism

INTRODUCTION

IN THIS CHAPTER I explore the impact of the conceit of androcentrism in the Buddhist traditions, leading to various forms of discrimination against women. Out of the different manifestations of superiority conceit that I have selected for study in this book, this is perhaps the one with the most detrimental repercussions for the Buddhist traditions as a whole. Just think of it: the potential of half of the Buddhist population is being stifled by obstructing women from taking leadership roles. This is such a waste of human resources and a cause of much unnecessary pain.

I begin with the problem of women being denied full participation in the monastic life and thereby the traditional avenue toward leadership positions. Such denial is an issue in particular in the Theravāda traditions, where a lineage of fully ordained women existed in the past and was subsequently lost. Its recent revival has created considerable controversies. In the Mahāyāna traditions of East Asia such a lineage has continued to exist until today and in the Himalayan traditions it never came into being, although this might change in the future.

In order to enable a proper appreciation of androcentric and at times even misogynistic attitudes toward women, in what follows I need to cover legal aspects of the question of full ordination in some detail. Although the first part of the present chapter thereby comes with a particular emphasis on the question of allowing women entry into the monastic order of the Theravāda traditions, certain attitudes taken up for study are, unfortunately, quite pervasive in all Buddhist traditions.

Another manifestation of androcentric conceit takes the form of assuming that the higher echelons of the path to awakening are the sole reserve of males, a tendency evident in relation to the path of the bodhi-sattva who aims to become a Buddha in the future. Such notions can be quite pervasive in different Buddhist traditions, whose exegetical traditions tend to presume that at an advanced point in the progress to Buddhahood the acquisition of a male body is an indispensable requirement.

In relation to both of these trajectories, my overall concern is to try to explain how certain historical conditions and developments have led to androcentrism, if not misogyny, in the hope that an understanding of the situation will provide the necessary foundation for a much-needed change.

1. NUNS

My presentation in the following pages can at times be somewhat dense, as I try to bring together and summarize complex developments and circumstances. As an easy way of introducing my topic, however, I begin here with a short story. This concerns a female disciple of a famous meditation teacher from Myanmar (Burma). Due to the unavailability of full ordination as a *bhikkhunī*, a fully ordained female monastic, she had taken the only ordination available to her in Myanmar, which involves observing eight or ten precepts and wearing a type of robes that differs visibly from those worn by fully ordained monastics. Such eight- or ten-precept nuns are found in different Theravāda countries, where they occupy an ambiguous position between the lay and the monastic world.

The nun of my story was running a meditation center on behalf of her teacher and had organized a retreat that he was going to lead. The teacher had come with a following of other *bhikkhus*, fully ordained male monastics, and everyone was very pleased that her organization and hard work had made things work smoothly for all participants.

According to the code of rules for monastics, the *Vinaya*, monastics are not permitted to help themselves to food on their own. In a traditional setting, the food will often be ceremoniously offered first to the most senior *bhikkhu*, who in this case was her teacher. The other *bhikkhus* then stand in a row behind the teacher and each in turn takes from the food. In this setting, the nun was the last to approach the table, due to her inferior hierarchical standing.

The food offered will usually involve a large amount of rice together with dishes with various curries and some sweets and fruits. When standing in the row, the practice is to keep an eye on how many monastics are behind oneself in order to make sure that one does not take too much of a particular food lest those at the end of the row no longer receive any of it.

Time and again during the retreat, the *bhikkhus* emptied all the dishes, and by the time the nun approached the table where the food was laid out, only rice was left. To use her own words, when she related this experience to me: "I only had my tears to go along with the plain rice."

The teacher and the *bhikkhus* were very appreciative of the nun; they had no intention to make her suffer in any way. But they simply did not perceive her as a monastic. Her in-between status made her appear as a lay person in the eyes of the *bhikkhus*. They failed to notice that someone else was behind them who also needed to be considered when they took food. The privilege of hierarchy prevented them from becoming aware of the impact of their actions.

Within the framework of the traditional form of relationship the nun had with her teacher, this was not something she could bring up explicitly with him or his *bhikkhus*. In an Asian setting, to do so would have been perceived as an inappropriate type of criticism and even an open challenge. As a monastic, it was also not appropriate for her to approach the lay donors and ask for additional food. In this way, even though she was the one who had organized the retreat and made everything go smoothly for the teacher and his following of *bhikkhus* as well as the other participants, much against her own wishes she was on a plain rice diet. The situation she experienced reflects the inequity resulting from her status as a nun who, in the eyes of tradition, is not really a full monastic but at the same time also no longer belongs to the laity.

The above episode is in line with various forms of daily discrimination toward women who have renounced lay life in Theravāda countries (Anālayo 2017i: 291–96). The main problem remains their ambiguous position between the lay and the monastic world. This in-between status can find reflection, for example, in the type of dress worn. The nuns of Myanmar often wear pinkish colored robes, a color never worn by *bhikkhus*, and the nuns of Thailand wear only white, similar to lay people on observance days. Nuns in both countries usually do not officiate at public ceremonies or preach in public. Whereas nuns in Sri Lanka take ten precepts, in Thailand they usually only take eight, another similarity to the practice of lay people on an observance day. The Thai government denies the nuns the right to vote, in line with the custom that monastics do not vote, but at the same time does not concede them the benefit of free travel on public transport, a privilege accorded to *bhikkhus*.

Not all nuns in Theravāda countries perceive their situation as discriminatory and some can at times be rather suspicious of feminist agendas, often perceived as foreign intrusions into a traditional religious world (Anālayo 2017g: 350–53). Nonetheless, they are certainly disadvantaged. A male wishing to go forth and live a monastic life can count on vastly superior opportunities, resources, and support, compared to a female wanting to do the same.

In view of this inequality, what are its historic roots? To what extent is such relegation of women to a second-class status in line with the viewpoint the canonical sources attribute to the historical Buddha?

In an attempt to explore how far androcentric forms of conceit are in conformity with or in opposition to the way the texts present the Buddha's own attitude, in what follows I first survey the historical and legal background to the question of *bhikkhunī* ordination in the Theravāda tradition. Then I will turn to the account of how the Buddha founded the order of *bhikkhunīs*.

2. DECLINE AND REVIVAL

From its homeland in India, the Buddhist monastic tradition was transmitted to Sri Lanka some two centuries after the time of the Buddha. According to the account given in a Sri Lankan chronicle, the arahant son of the Indian king Asoka, the *bhikkhu* Mahinda, had successfully converted the royal family of Sri Lanka (Anālayo 2018a: 202–10). When he was requested to grant the going forth to become a *bhikkhunī* to the queen and a group of her female followers, Mahinda refused. According to his explanation, in the way this is recorded in the Sri Lankan chronicle, he first needed to have *bhikkhunīs* come from India in order to collaborate with him and other *bhikkhu*s in giving ordination to female candidates.

As a basic principle of monastic law, granting ordination requires a group of already-ordained monastics. For the ordination to be valid, these monastics need to perform the actual ordination in accordance with the stipulations made in the relevant legal text, the *Vinaya*. Buddhist monastic traditions are based on the execution of legal acts in communal harmony and nobody is invested with the power to issue new laws. Only the Buddha had the authority to pronounce rules and regulations, which remain binding for subsequent generations of monastics. These parameters need to be kept in mind when evaluating the granting of full ordination to women.

In the case of Sri Lanka, a group of *bhikkhunīs* headed by Mahinda's sister, the *bhikkhunī* Saṅghamittā, came from India to Sri Lanka to ordain the queen and her followers and thereby transmit the *bhikkhunī* ordination lineage. At some time in the early eleventh century, during a period of warfare and political turmoil, the order of *bhikkhunīs* in Sri Lanka disappeared. Several centuries earlier, the same had happened in India.

At a still earlier time, however, in the early fifth century, *bhikkhunīs* from Sri Lanka travelled to China and participated in ordinations there (Anālayo 2018b: 125–27). Due to the absence of a group of *bhikkhus* ordained in the same *Vinaya* tradition, what took place at that time in China could not have been a full transmission of Theravāda *bhikkhunī* ordination. For a full transmission, a collaboration of *bhikkhus* and *bhikkhunīs* ordained according to the same monastic code would have been required.

In the eighth century the *Vinaya* of a Buddhist tradition known as Dharmaguptaka was imposed by imperial decree on all monastics in China. This is the *Vinaya* still followed today in countries like China, Korea, and Vietnam. Its code of rules for monastics differs from the Theravāda *Vinaya*; regulations on how to conduct ordination also vary in several respects. This in turn means that someone ordained in one of these two *Vinaya* traditions cannot grant ordination that will be recognized as legally valid by all members of the other tradition. This holds regardless of whether the candidate is male or female.

Returning to Sri Lanka, when in the early eleventh century the order of *bhikkhunīs* came to an end, to the best of our knowledge in other parts of the world there were no *bhikkhunīs*, ordained according to Theravāda law, who could have been brought to Sri Lanka to grant ordination. Since then, the option of taking full ordination has no longer been available to women in Theravāda countries. This explains the coming into existence of traditions of nuns who take only eight or ten precepts instead of following a full monastic code of rules and who wear robes that differ from those worn by *bhikkhus* and *bhikkhunīs*.

In recent times, however, several attempts at reviving the Theravāda order of *bhikkhunīs* have taken place in Thailand and Sri Lanka. Following ordinations held in 1998 in India and Sri Lanka, the order of *bhikkhunīs* has been steadily growing in Sri Lanka and also taken root in Thailand. The first group of Sri Lankan candidates received ordination twice, once in a ceremony that involved the collaboration of Chinese monastics ordained according to the Dharmaguptaka *Vinaya*, and again in another ceremony carried out by Theravāda *bhikkhus* on their own. This double ordination has strengthened the appeal to legal validity of the revival of the Theravāda order of *bhikkhunīs* and has empowered its subsequent growth.

3. THE LEGAL PROBLEM

A proper appreciation of the revival of *bhikkhunī* ordination requires awareness of the legal complexities involved. The question is not merely one of patriarchal resistance to allowing women their rightful place, although such attitudes can at times play a role. Here, it can be helpful to distinguish between those concerned with proper adherence to the procedures of the *Vinaya* and those who are in principle opposed to the revival of *bhikkhunī* ordination for a range of reasons.

By way of premise, the right of a religious tradition to maintain its customs and observances needs to be given due recognition. The Theravāda traditions of South and Southeast Asia have been deeply influenced by the perceived need to protect themselves against Western colonial domination and more recently against the disintegrating forces of secularism, similarly seen as driven predominantly by the West. In view of this historical precedent, reviving a *bhikkhunī* order in ways that openly conflict with basic Theravāda legal principles can easily be seen as the shadow of past colonial arrogance and the continuation of the disintegrating influences of secularization that threaten to destroy local religious practices and observances.

Theravāda *bhikkhus* who are concerned with a strict interpretation and implementation of their *Vinaya* will not recognize the ordination of a *bhikkhu* done in ways that openly conflict with their understanding of the parameters of a valid ordination. These require the proper demarcation of the space for the ordination ritual, the adoption of the Pāli language for the ordination formula, and the congregation of a certain number of validly ordained *bhikkhus* to confer the ordination, just to mention some key aspects. An ordination that involves monastics who are ordained according to a different *Vinaya*, for example, has little chance of being recognized.

For this reason, if a Theravāda ordination is performed in collaboration with monastics ordained according to the Dharmaguptaka *Vinaya*, it is unreasonable to expect that this will be considered valid from a Theravāda legal viewpoint. Reservations against such an ordination need to be seen for what they are, namely objections to certain procedures that would be raised regardless of whether those ordained in this way are males or females.

4. A LEGAL SOLUTION

The involvement of monastics ordained according to the Dharmaguptaka *Vinaya* is not the only possible way to proceed for reviving the extinct Theravāda *bhikkhunī* order. A close perusal of the Pāli *Vinaya* shows that it is in principle possible for *bhikkhus* to ordain women on their own when no order of *bhikkhunīs* is in existence to collaborate with them in granting ordination to female candidates (Anālayo 2018a). This solution requires a brief look at the history of *bhikkhunī* ordination as described in the Theravāda *Vinaya*.

The first relevant promulgation by the Buddha takes the form of eight weighty principles, *garudhamma* (translated by Bodhi 2012: 1190). According to the narrative setting, the Buddha made the acceptance of these eight weighty principles the way of granting ordination to his foster mother, Mahāpajāpatī Gotamī. Although the authenticity of these weighty principles has at times been doubted, this impression is not confirmed by a comparative study (Anālayo 2016b: 95–116). Instead, the basic idea that the Buddha made some such foundational stipulations appears to be as historical as other aspects found in common among the different *Vinaya* accounts of the establishment of the order of *bhikkhunīs*.

According to the Theravāda *Vinaya*, one of these weighty principles stipulates that a woman who wishes to receive full ordination should go through a training period and receive ordination from both orders, the order of *bhikkhus* and the order of *bhikkhunīs*. The depiction in the Theravāda *Vinaya* of the Buddha asking Mahāpajāpatī to accept this particular weighty principle involves a double bind. In order to become a *bhikkhunī* herself, she had to agree to a procedure for ordaining other female candidates that at that time was impossible to put into practice. Forming an order of *bhikkhunīs* to collaborate with an order of *bhikkhus* to grant ordination to female candidates requires the existence of other *bhikkhunīs* who could join Mahāpajāpatī to constitute such an order. As a single *bhikkhunī*, she could not form an order and thereby was unable to fulfill the stipulation made in the weighty principle. The way this weighty principle is formulated in the Theravāda *Vinaya* actually prevented the granting of ordination to her five hundred followers, who also wanted to go forth.

It seems fairly implausible that the *Vinaya* account here depicts the Buddha as having just overlooked the obvious consequences of his own promulgation. Instead, from an emic perspective the ensuing dilemma is probably best read as conveying something done on purpose, in the sense of creating a situation that permits additional legislation.

Predictably in fact, the *Vinaya* continues with the report that Mahāpajāpatī asked how to proceed in regard to her followers. In response, the Buddha is on record as promulgating a rule that *bhikkhus* can give ordination to women on their own. This authorization, relevant to a situation when no *bhikkhunī* order is in existence, has never been explicitly revoked and can therefore be relied on in the current situation to revive the order of *bhikkhunīs* (Anālayo 2018a: 184–200).

The legal situation that emerges from the Theravāda *Vinaya* provides the background required for appreciating events in Sri Lanka. Mahinda's refusal to ordain the queen of Sri Lanka and her followers is understandable, since at that time there were *bhikkhunīs* in existence in India who could be brought to Sri Lanka for granting ordination. Given the precedent set by Mahinda, however, it seems fairly probable that in later times, when the order of *bhikkhunīs* had disappeared, the *bhikkhus* would have assumed that it is in principle impossible for them to ordain *bhikkhunīs* on their own. The words of the arahant Mahinda, renowned for his central role in the spread of Buddhism to Sri Lanka, must have been held in deep respect and would simply have been followed. Any consultation of the *Vinaya* would have had that viewpoint as its starting point and led to the assumption that the permission for *bhikkhus* to ordain *bhikkhunīs* on their own was no longer valid, as to grant such an ordination requires the collaboration of both orders.

This would explain why traditional Theravāda *bhikkhus* throughout the centuries appear to have been living with the sincere belief that it is not possible to revive an order of *bhikkhunīs*, once it has become defunct. From such a viewpoint, it is in principle impossible for *bhikkhus* to do so on their own, and it can also not be done in collaboration with *bhikkhunīs* who follow a different *Vinaya*. In particular the latter option, due to the perceived need to protect traditional Theravāda customs and observances, has invested the whole issue with a considerable emotional charge. As a result, Theravāda *bhikkhunīs* still lack official recognition and are subject to various forms of discrimination, even though the revival of their order is in principle a legally valid option.

5. Apprehensions

An opposition of traditional Theravāda *bhikkhus* to what they perceive as a violation of the basic principles of their monastic code needs to be differentiated from other motivations. In fact, those who are not under the influence of such motivations often show themselves open to evaluating seriously the above-mentioned legal solution. This solution requires reconsidering the relevant part of the *Vinaya* on its own, setting aside the traditional perspective that has been influencing the matter for centuries, in order to appreciate that the permission for *bhikkhus* to ordain female candidates without the collaboration of an order of *bhikkhunīs* is a valid option for reviving such an order.

A willingness to allow for a shift of perspective, as long as it remains within the legal parameters of Theravāda law, will not be an option for those who are in principle committed to keeping women out of the monastic order and thus in a subordinate position. Here a wholesale rejection of the validity of *bhikkhunī* ordination appears as the only acceptable position. Such attitudes can conveniently be illustrated by turning to attempts by Bhikkhu Ṭhānissaro to refute the legality of a revival of *bhikkhunī* ordination. Elsewhere I have replied to the main points adduced (Anālayo 2015c, 2017h, 2018c, and 2019l: 61–67), hence in what follows I concentrate on the type of attitude that can inform such a dismissal of the revival of the *bhikkhunī* order.

A Buddhist society should ideally be based on the smooth collaboration of four types of members, who are male or female and lay or monastic. Since in the Theravāda traditions women do not have access to full ordination, they are not able to realize their full potential in contributing to such collaboration among the four assemblies. Such collaboration could be compared to the four legs of a noble elephant, each leg representing one of the four assemblies. On adopting this comparison, the situation in the current Theravāda traditions is similar to the elephant having one leg crippled (Anālayo 2014a: 16). The elephant can still walk, but only with difficulty. Similarly, a Buddhist tradition that lacks an order of *bhikkhunīs* and has only three of the four assemblies continues only with difficulty. The crippled leg, reflecting the ambiguous position of Theravāda nuns in between the monastic and the lay world, can be restored to full functionality by reviving *bhikkhunī* ordination. In reply to this illustration, Ṭhānissaro (2015: 23) presents the following reinterpretation of the simile:

> the analogy is inaccurate. A more accurate analogy would be this: The religion is like an elephant with a severed leg. A doctor wants to reattach the leg, even though it has long been dead, and his tools for doing so are contaminated. If the operation goes forward, it will hasten the elephant's death.

The change of the crippled leg into a severed one implies a wholesale dismissal of eight- and ten-precept nuns as something dead that no longer has a living connection to the Buddha's dispensation. The reinterpretation also entails that granting women the place the Buddha originally accorded to them involves a lethal contamination. Its ultimate result will be to hasten the end of the whole tradition, corresponding to the death of the elephant.

The stark impression created in this way suggests the influence of deep-seated anxieties and apprehensions. It can safely be assumed that resistance to the revival of *bhikkhunī* ordination is in this case not merely based on legal considerations. More appears to be at stake.

Associating women with contamination can be particularly prominent in the Theravāda tradition of Thailand, due to the influence of local menstruation taboos. According to Thai custom, a *bhikkhu* is expected to avoid receiving anything given by a woman directly and instead should put out a piece of cloth on which the offering is to be placed. Departure from such behavior will likely be seen by others as a sign of the bad morality of the *bhikkhu* in question. In the northeast of Thailand, menstruation phobia goes so far as to result in prohibiting women from entry at any time into the monastic buildings in which the *bhikkhus* periodically congregate to carry out legal acts (Anālayo 2017i: 160–61). An example is the signboard shown in figure 1.

Besides reflecting a cultural conditioning in Thai Theravāda Buddhism, in a way the signboard also enshrines the basic attitude evident

ห้ามผู้หญิงขึ้น

THIS PLACE IS FORBIDDEN
FOR WOMEN

Figure 1. Signboard at the entrance to the *uposatha* hall,
Wat Phra That Sri Chomtong, Chiang Mai.

in the reinterpretation of the elephant analogy, in that the institution of Buddhist monasticism becomes a place that is in principle forbidden for women.

The impression such attitudes can evoke in those denied the right to take full ordination can be illustrated by the following reflections by the former nun Thanissara (2015: 67):

> Basically, as they would say in the British army, we weren't up to muster. This was a men's club, and they would make the rules, and those rules would always keep us as women in an ambivalent, disempowered, and dependent state. At any cost, those rules would defend against the amorphous, rolling tides of the feminine, which destabilized men and left them feeling vulnerable and out of control.

6. THE PREDICTION OF DECLINE

In his writings against the legality of *bhikkhunī* ordination, Ṭhānissaro (2018: 50) arrives at the verdict that "for the long life of the Dhamma and Vinaya, we will have to leave the Trojan horse outside." The image of the Trojan horse here represents the revival of *bhikkhunī* ordination. The perceived need to protect the long life of the Dhamma and Vinaya points to the influence of the prediction of decline that, according to the Pāli *Vinaya* account, the Buddha gave after he had granted ordination to his foster mother and thereby taken the decisive step in founding an order of *bhikkhunīs*.

This prediction states that, due to the coming into existence of *bhikkhunīs*, the lifetime of the Buddha's dispensation has been halved: it will endure only five hundred years instead of a thousand. Here is the actual formulation from the Theravāda *Vinaya*, in which the term "Tathāgata" stands for the Buddha (Anālayo 2016b: 233):

> Since women have gone forth from home to homelessness in
> the teaching and discipline made known by the Tathāgata,
> now the holy life will not endure long, the right teaching will
> now remain [only] for five hundred years.

This contrasts to a duration of a thousand years if women had not received the going forth, hence my supplementation of "only" in the translation. Needless to say, with a history of some two thousand five hundred years, the Buddhist traditions have outlived both time periods mentioned in this prediction.

According to Ṭhānissaro (2018: 28), however, the prediction attributed to the Buddha "was actually quite prescient, in that it was approximately 500 years after his death that the Prajñāpāramitā Sūtras first appeared." This claim equates the Perfection of Wisdom texts with a decline of the Dharma. As the comment by Bhikkhu Ṭhānissaro illustrates, facing clear evidence that the predicted decline did not come to pass will prompt a need to devise alternative explanations. The Pāli commentarial tradition attempts to achieve this by reinterpreting the reference to five hundred years to mean five thousand years (Nattier 1991: 56–58 and Endo 2004). The implausibility of the commentarial suggestion may have motivated Bhikkhu Ṭhānissaro to refer to the Perfection of Wisdom texts as an alternative strategy, putting the blame on scriptures other Buddhist traditions consider sacred.

Would it not be more reasonable to set this prediction of decline aside as something that evidently has not come true? What is it that invests this particular passage with such strong influence among a sizeable number of male Buddhist monastics, an influence not confined to members of the Theravāda traditions?

7. Problems with the Prediction of Decline

The challenge of understanding why the prediction of decline continues to have such a powerful influence goes beyond the mere fact that it has turned out not to be true. If the institution of an order of *bhikkhunīs* really had such detrimental consequences, it is difficult to understand why the Buddha took such a step in the first place.

The Pāli *Vinaya* reports that the Buddha's attendant Ānanda intervened on behalf of Mahāpajāpatī Gotamī's quest for ordination, reminding the Buddha of his debt of gratitude to her. She had suckled him after his mother had passed away, soon after his birth. A Pāli discourse reports the same argument made by Ānanda on another occasion, when Mahāpajāpatī Gotamī wanted to offer the Buddha a robe (translated by Ñāṇamoli 1995/2005: 1102). On that occasion the Buddha refused to accept the robe, even after this argument was made. This makes it hardly conceivable that the same argument was sufficiently strong to make him change his mind regarding the founding of an order of *bhikkhunīs*. In fact, the Buddha had already settled that debt of gratitude by giving her teachings that led her to stream entry, the first of the four levels of awakening.

Not only does Ānanda's reminder of the debt of gratitude not explain why the Buddha would take a step that presumably results in dramatically shortening the lifespan of his teaching. It is even more perplexing that in the Pāli *Vinaya* account the Buddha only mentions these devastating consequences when it is too late. He first stipulates the acceptance of the weighty principles as the way for Mahāpajāpatī Gotamī to become a *bhikkhunī*. After she has accepted and Ānanda returns to report this, the Buddha replies with the prediction of decline. At this point, nothing can be done any more to prevent the predicted decline. This stands in contrast to other passages describing future decline of the teachings, which regularly come with explicit indications of the type of practice and conduct that will prevent that decline (Anālayo 2019g: 131).

In addition to such narrative inconsistencies, the very idea that the institution of an order of *bhikkhunīs* is detrimental to the Buddhist dispensation flies in the face of a range of other passages in Pāli discourses (Anālayo 2018a: 28–52). These indicate that the Buddha had made a firm resolution not to pass away until he had competent disciples in each of the four assemblies (translated by Walshe 1987: 246, Bodhi 2000: 1724, Bodhi 2012: 1214, and Ireland 1990: 87). One of these four is the assembly of *bhikkhunīs*, the other three are the assemblies of *bhikkhus*, male lay followers, and female lay followers. Without enabling women to go forth and become *bhikkhunīs*, this aspiration of the Buddha could not have been fulfilled. It would have been impossible for him to have competent *bhikkhunī* disciples without first allowing an order of *bhikkhunīs* to come into existence.

Another discourse relates the completeness of the Buddha's teaching to the accomplishment reached by each of the four assemblies of disciples, including *bhikkhunīs* who are senior, of middle standing, and recently ordained (translated by Walshe 1987: 431). How could such completeness ever have been reached without first granting women the opportunity to become *bhikkhunīs*?

Still another relevant passage concerns auspicious bodily marks of the Buddha, which already at his birth served as portents of various endowments and qualities to be expected of him, once he had become a Buddha. One of these is a wheel mark on the soles of his feet, which portends his being surrounded by many disciples, including *bhikkhunīs* (translated by Walshe 1987: 444). From the perspective of this passage, it was impossible for the Buddha not to start an order of *bhikkhunīs* at some point in his career.

Several passages more directly relate to future decline (translated by Bodhi 2000: 681 and Bodhi 2012: 818, 904, and 1058). Such a decline can be prevented through appropriate conduct by *bhikkhus*, *bhikkhunīs*, male lay followers, and female lay followers. Here the *bhikkhunīs*, provided they adopt the required conduct, contribute to preventing decline rather than causing it.

Considering this large number of textual references standing in direct contrast to the prediction of decline, together with the narrative inconsistencies it creates in the Pāli *Vinaya*, and the fact that it never came to pass, the success of this prediction in influencing attitudes among some male monastics must be occurring on an irrational level. Its appeal is not because it can lay a claim to being reasonable or an authentic record of the Buddha's attitude. Instead, its appeal appears to be due to a resonance on the level of unconscious attitudes and assumptions. For this reason, it tends to be picked out of all relevant passages as the only relevant one, ignoring those that are dissonant with it.

8. After the Buddha's Demise

The prediction of decline, found in the Pāli *Vinaya*, can also be examined with the help of a comparative study of its different versions. Since such study is of considerable relevance for this and subsequent chapters, here I briefly sketch the basic methodological principles involved. The discourses and *Vinaya* extant in Pāli are the final products of centuries of oral transmission of texts believed to have been spoken originally by the Buddha and his disciples. These orally transmitted texts eventually reached Sri Lanka and were committed to writing about four centuries after the time when the Buddha must have lived.

Other Buddhist traditions in India similarly preserved their records of the Buddha's teachings and these were eventually also written down. With the disappearance of Buddhism from India, much of the material from these other Buddhist traditions was lost. Fortunately, by that time collections of discourses and *Vinayas* had been brought to China and translated into Chinese; a few discourses and the *Vinaya* of one tradition also reached Tibet and were translated into Tibetan. In addition to these translations, relevant material has also been preserved in manuscripts that primarily come from Central Asia.

Recourse to parallels to the Pāli discourses and *Vinaya* makes it possible to compare different versions of a particular text and to rectify transmission errors. It enables identifying the "early Buddhist" perspective on a particular matter, corresponding roughly to the period from the fifth to the third century before the Common Era.

Of significance for the present topic is the *Vinaya* account of the first *saṅgīti*, a term that stands for a "communal recitation" (less adequately translated as "council;" see Tilakaratna 2000). This was according to the traditional account held by senior *bhikkhus* soon after the Buddha's passing away. Comparative study of the relevant passage in different *Vinaya*s makes it in my view probable that the prediction of decline emerged during the oral transmission of accounts of this communal recitation (Anālayo 2016b: 159–77 and 2019l: 75n87).

Concerns regarding how to ensure the survival of the Buddhist tradition, after the passing away of its founder, would naturally have led to shoring up institutional identity in such a way that public opinion could be won over and continuous support be ensured. In view of the subordinate position of women in mainstream ancient Indian society, an order of *bhikkhunīs* could easily have been perceived as problematic. Apprehensions of possible decline were presumably simply projected onto the *bhikkhunīs*. Such apprehensions appear to have eventually been attributed to the arahant Mahākassapa, an eminent disciple of the Buddha who in the *Vinaya* narrative functions as the convener of the communal recitation. The episode in question portrays Mahākassapa in dialogue with Ānanda. The overall report of their interaction appears to personify two currents among the *bhikkhu* disciples: the Buddha's attendant Ānanda represents an inclusive attitude, whereas the portrayal of Mahākassapa reflects an exclusive attitude.

Given that the account of this dialogue is found in the same *Vinaya* text as the story of the founding of the order of *bhikkhunīs*, in the context of oral transmission it does not take much for a negative evaluation to shift to another dialogue that also involves Ānanda and is situated at an earlier point in narrative time. Such a shift could have resulted in attributing those apprehensions to the one who in this earlier episode is in dialogue with Ānanda, namely to the Buddha himself rather than to Mahākassapa. Although this remains a hypothesis, in this way an opinion that would have originated among some *bhikkhu*s responsible for the transmission of the account of the first communal recitation could have been successively attributed to Mahākassapa and then to the Buddha himself.

9. The Buddha's Refusal

The prediction of decline is not the only negative element in the account of the founding of an order of *bhikkhunīs*. Another such element is the Buddha's initial refusal to grant ordination to Mahāpajāpatī Gotamī and her followers. On consulting the Pāli *Vinaya* version of this refusal, the impression can easily arise that the Buddha indeed did not want to have an order of *bhikkhunīs*.

Comparative study of the parallels again provides a helpful perspective. Several versions report that the Buddha's refusal was accompanied by an alternative suggestion. This was for Mahāpajāpatī Gotamī and her followers to shave their heads and wear monastic robes—but stay at home (Anālayo 2016b: 49–52).

The implication seems to be that at this early stage in the development of Buddhist monasticism, with a dearth of proper accommodation and other resources, it would have been preferable for Mahāpajāpatī Gotamī and her followers not to embark on the life of wandering mendicants. In particular for women, apparently perceived by some members of the Indian male population as a commodity to satisfy their sexual urges, going forth would have made them vulnerable to abuse. The Pāli *Vinaya* indeed reports several cases of rape of *bhikkhunīs* (Anālayo 2016b: 125–29). This indication is in line with what we know of the ancient Indian setting, where women not protected by their husbands risked being seen by lecherous males as a commodity without an owner.

When evaluated against this background, for the Buddha to hesitate in permitting his own foster mother and her followers to embark on the life of wandering mendicants becomes understandable. This in turn would imply that the Buddha was not in principle against starting an order of *bhikkhunīs*, an attitude that is also evident in the various passages surveyed above. Instead, his initial refusal may have been motivated by apprehension that the time was not yet ripe for such a move.

The absence in some *Vinayas* of a proposal by the Buddha that Mahāpajāpatī Gotamī and her followers could shave their heads and wear monastic robes may in turn be a case of textual loss. This suggestion receives corroboration from the ensuing narrative in those *Vinayas* that do not contain this episode; these report that Mahāpajāpatī Gotamī and her followers did indeed shave their heads and don robes (Anālayo 2016b: 54–57). Seeing them with shaven heads and in robes, neither Ānanda nor the Buddha show any sign of surprise at this action. Had Mahāpajāpatī Gotamī and her followers done this without some permission given previously by the Buddha, it would have been an act of open defiance. Such an act would have provoked comments if not censure. From the viewpoint of this narrative, the absence of any reaction of this type makes it fair to consider the alternative proposal found in other accounts to be probably an early element in the story of the formation of the order of *bhikkhunīs*. According to this alternative proposal, women would have been permitted to live a monastic life with the proviso that, for the time being, they did so in the protected environment of their homes.

10. NARRATIVE STRATEGIES OF DEVALUATION

The apparent loss of the alternative suggested by the Buddha results in presenting his attitude in a different light. Instead of reflecting a concern to protect women from abuse, he appears just unwilling to allow them to enter the monastic order. The attitude conveyed in this way can be exemplified with a sculpture from Gandhāra shown in figure 2.

If the identification of its import is correct, the image combines two episodes into a single scene, a common procedure in ancient Indian art. Since the women on the right side of the Buddha wear lay clothes, they would represent Mahāpajāpatī Gotamī and her followers at the time of making their initial request, before they shaved their heads and donned robes. The *bhikkhu* standing to the left of the Buddha would then be Ānanda, whose intervention belongs to the second episode, when Mahāpajāpatī

Figure 2. Gandhāran sculpture probably depicting the request
to found an order of *bhikkhunī*s.

Gotamī and her followers would no longer have been wearing lay clothes.
Of particular interest is the depiction of the Buddha. Although the face
is damaged, it can still be seen that he does not look at Mahāpajāpatī
Gotamī, and the overall impression is one of refusal, standing in contrast
to the reverential attitude of the women.

This aspect of the Gandhāran sculpture corresponds to narrative strategies of distancing women. The employment of such strategies can be
exemplified with the *Nandakovāda-sutta*, a discourse that reports teachings given to Mahāpajāpatī Gotamī and a group of *bhikkhunī*s (translated
by Ñāṇamoli 1995/2005: 1120). Comparison of the Pāli version with two
parallels from related transmission lineages, extant in Chinese translation, shows several differences (Anālayo 2016b: 15–38).

In the Pāli version the followers of Mahāpajāpatī are just referred to as
"five hundred *bhikkhunī*s," whereas the parallels introduce them by name
and qualify them as great disciples. According to the Pāli report, Mahāpajāpatī remains standing and asks the Buddha for a teaching, a request the
Buddha does not grant. In fact, throughout the Pāli account the Buddha
never directly speaks to her or her followers. In the two parallels, however,
Mahāpajāpatī instead sits down, and even without having been requested
to do so, the Buddha gives her a teaching.

After Mahāpajāpatī Gotamī and her followers have twice received teachings from a *bhikkhu* called Nandaka, the Pāli version reports the attainment of stream entry or higher levels of awakening by the *bhikkhunīs* after the second teaching. In the two parallels, however, already with the first teaching the *bhikkhunīs* reach nonreturn, the third level of awakening. With the second teaching, they all become fully awakened.

Closer inspection brings to light indications that the Pāli version has incorporated later elements. In other words, this does not appear to be an embellishment of the story on the side of the parallels, but much rather a case of a change for the worse on the side of the Pāli discourse (Anālayo 2019l: 54–58).

Needless to say, such narrative strategies are found not only in Pāli texts, but similarly manifest in the texts of other reciter traditions. The employment of such strategies in the present case shows how a story of success can gradually come to convey quite a different message.

The same is probably true of the story of the founding of the order of *bhikkhunīs*. An original element of this story would have been an explicit affirmation, still found in one way or another in all versions, that women can indeed reach all levels of awakening (Anālayo 2016b: 76–79). This provides a self-evident rationale for the Buddha's allowing them to enter the monastic life, with the initial proviso that it is preferable for the time being if they do not adopt a mendicant life. The original story would also have endorsed women's agency, since it is on Mahāpajāpatī Gotamī's initiative that she and her followers acquire full monastic status.

11. Ancient Roots of Misogyny

The tendency to present *bhikkhunīs* in particular and women in general in a negative light goes further than just the employment of narrative strategies of devaluation. Several discourses extant in Pāli show that misogyny in Buddhism has ancient roots (Anālayo 2016b: 140–45), reflecting attitudes that also manifest in one way or another in discourses of other transmission lineages. A shared characteristic of such discourses tends to be the absence of parallels. Such instances appear to reflect attitudes prevalent among later generations of those responsible for transmitting the respective textual collections.

According to relevant Pāli passages, women never have enough of sex and giving birth (translated by Bodhi 2012: 168); they are angry, envious, greedy, and without wisdom (translated by Bodhi 2012: 465). Betrayal of friends is one of the five dangers in women, the other four being that they are dirty, smelly, frightening, and dangerous; hence they are comparable to black snakes (translated by Bodhi 2012: 830). In fact, nearly all women not only betray friends but are also slanderous, very passionate, and adulterous (translated by Bodhi 2012: 830).

The passages mentioned above are found in the Collection of Numerical Discourses. Bhikkhu Bodhi (2012: 60–62) comments:

> a small number of discourses in the collection testify to a misogynistic attitude that strikes us as discordant, distasteful, and simply unjustified . . . in a text like AN [the Collection of Numerical Discourses], with its many short suttas, it would have been relatively easy for monks, apprehensive about their own sexuality . . . to insert such passages into the canon . . . quite in contrast to the suttas with a misogynistic tone are others that show the Buddha acting cordially toward women and generously bestowing his teaching upon them . . . it is hard to reconcile such texts, which display a friendly and empathetic attitude toward women, with the passages that categorically denigrate their capacities.

It seems indeed hard, if not impossible, to reconcile such texts with the Buddha's attitude toward women reflected in the remainder of the texts. None of these discourses has a parallel in the extant discourse collections of other traditions, although the comparison of women's five bad qualities with a snake recurs in a later Buddhist text (Anālayo 2016b: 142). Notably, in that text some young men have misattributed this comparison to the Buddha. When women hear about it and approach the Buddha, knowing what is on their minds he instead expounds to them five virtues in women and then gives them a teaching resulting in their stream entry.

This episode can well be taken to exemplify the pattern that quite probably stands behind such passages. Although misogynist statements are at times attributed to the Buddha, they are best set aside as not being accurate records of his attitude toward and assessment of women. Instead, they must be reflecting the influence of views held in the ancient Indian setting among those involved in transmitting the texts. Some of the misogynist ideas in such discourses also occur in a legal text of ancient India that postdates the time of the Buddha, the *Manusmṛti* (Olivelle 2004: 156). In the words of Collett (2018: 559),

> the idea of women being inferior comes from the notion that female nature is the problem, and . . . the negativity towards women and sporadic misogyny we come across in Pāli literature has likely found its way in via ingestion of the traditional (non-Buddhist) view of women found in ancient South Asian societies, rather than for a doctrinally motivated or ethically significant reason grounded in Buddhist principles or teaching.

Relevant to assessing such statements is also the underlying premise that categorical statements can be made about women in general. This contrasts with the position taken by the Buddha according to other discourses, which show him time and again eschewing unilateral statements in favor of introducing finer distinctions based on an analytical approach. His attitude in this respect manifests repeatedly in relation to unqualified claims based on caste. Countering assumptions that a brahmin, by dint of birth, is inherently superior to members of other castes, the texts show the Buddha consistently taking the position that moral conduct and mental qualities overrule birth. This holds for any type of discrimination based on qualities that come with birth and therefore equally applies to biological sex (and of course also to race; Anālayo 2020b).

In sum, it seems fair to conclude, with Sponberg (1992: 20–21), that as an expression of

> a fear of the feminine, and a fear specifically of its power to undermine male celibacy . . . the emergence of conventional

misogyny into Buddhist literature would represent a shift in perspective away from the psychological soteriology of the earliest tradition back toward the purification soteriology of the ascetics who had been criticized for their excesses by Śākyamuni.

The same ascetic ideology informs the prediction of decline, which shares with the passages surveyed above the adoption of a categorical stance based on birth. Rather than decline being the result of bad moral conduct or unwholesome mental attitudes, as evident in other passages related to this topic, the entry of women into the monastic domain spells decline. This idea is based on an essentialized notion of womanhood that does not leave room for individual distinctions. It thereby stands in contrast to the importance accorded in early Buddhist texts to individual responsibility and an ethics of the mind.

12. POSITIVE IMAGES OF WOMEN

A reflection of the normative early Buddhist attitude toward such essentializing of womanhood can be found in an episode that involves the celestial Māra and an accomplished *bhikkhunī*. In early Buddhist discourse, a prominent role of Māra is to personify problems posed by external events as well as outsiders to members of the Buddhist community, including the Buddha himself. The Māra motif thereby has the didactic role of providing a model of how such challenges are best faced. This finds illustration in the exemplary way in which the Buddha or his disciples rebuff Māra (Anālayo 2015d: 201–5).

In the episode in question, Māra voices the presumption that women's insufficient wisdom prevents them from reaching the state of a sage (translated by Bodhi 2000: 222). Notably, this is the only instance in the early discourses in which women's ability to reach awakening is called into question. The fact that the speaker is Māra makes it clear that such a suggestion, far from being seriously entertained, should be seen as merely one of his silly pranks.

The accomplished *bhikkhunī* faced with this challenge is not short of a reply. She queries how womanhood could possibly be relevant once the

mind is concentrated and endowed with knowledge. Māra would do better to go and challenge those who still identify with being a woman or a
man. On hearing this response, Māra realizes that he has been defeated
and vanishes.

This instance neatly exemplifies how essentialized notions of womanhood and categorical statements about a woman's supposed bad qualities
fail to make sense from the viewpoint of a mind accomplished in concentration and wisdom. Reaching the state of a sage depends on moral conduct and meditative practice, not on the type of body acquired at birth.

The above episode concerned with women's spiritual abilities is one
in altogether ten encounters between Māra and accomplished *bhikkhunīs*, and in each case he has to leave the scene in defeat (Anālayo 2015d:
201–34). Several of his challenges involve some form of sexual invitation
or even threat. This stands in contrast to a single instance in the same
body of texts where Māra's daughters pose a sexual challenge, in this case
trying to tempt the Buddha (translated by Bodhi 2000: 217). This goes to
show that early Buddhist texts do not unilaterally consider women to be
Māra's forces who lure innocent males into sexual indulgence. Instead, it
is the *male* Māra who represents sensual temptation and sexual aggres-
sion, and those who remain completely uninterested are ordained women.
Although this does not necessarily hold for later traditions, in the early
Buddhist discourses the tendency to make sexual advances appears to be
more prominently related to males than to females.

In addition to the set of ten discourses with accomplished *bhikkhunīs* rebuffing Māra, several other passages also throw into relief the high
degree of realization reached by Buddhist women who went forth. Unlike
the misogynist passages surveyed earlier, these discourses tend to be well
represented in different transmission lineages and can for this reason
be considered better testimonies to early Buddhist thought. One such
instance reports that over five hundred *bhikkhunīs* had reached full awakening, and the same number of lay women had reached the second highest
stage of awakening (translated by Ñāṇamoli 1995/2005: 596). Although
the number five hundred tends to carry a symbolic value in the early discourses, it nevertheless implies that there were large numbers of highly
realized women, both ordained and lay.

Given that most of the early discourses are explicitly addressed to *bhikkhus*, the impression could arise that male monastics were the sole audience to which the teachings in question were directed. This is not the case, however, as the mode of address employed in these texts reflects ancient protocols of conversation (Collett and Anālayo 2014). The same custom can also take the form of addressing a group of friends by the name of their leader, whose name will for this purpose be put into the plural. An example is when the Buddha addresses his disciple Anuruddha and his friends by saying "Anuruddhas." Just as this formulation is not meant to address Anuruddha alone, the address "*bhikkhus*" is also not meant to restrict the teachings to fully ordained male monastics.

The discourses report the Buddha upholding two *bhikkhunīs* as models for other ordained women and two female lay disciples as models for other lay women (translated by Bodhi 2000: 689 and 2012: 179). One *bhikkhunī* was apparently such an extraordinary speaker that even a sprite toured the town to reprove those who did not come to listen to her teachings (translated by Bodhi 2000: 313). Another *bhikkhunī* is on record as giving dexterous replies to a series of profound and intricate questions in such a way that the Buddha declared he would have answered those questions in just the same way (translated by Ñāṇamoli 1995/2005: 403). Her profound explanations have served as a continuous source of inspiration for later generations (Anālayo 2012b: 61).

Several *bhikkhunīs* and lay women are acclaimed as outstanding for praiseworthy qualities and forms of conduct (translated by Bodhi 2012: 111). Proper appreciation of this description requires taking into account that, if a particular *bhikkhunī* or lay woman was regarded as outstanding among *bhikkhunīs* or female lay disciples in a certain quality or conduct, it follows that she was not the only one in this category (Anālayo 2016a: 321–24). There must have been a number of women who had gained the quality mentioned or were endowed with the conduct described, and among these the one mentioned explicitly stood out as exemplary. The fame of these eminent disciples has also kept inspiring subsequent generation. An example is a mural depiction in Pagan, shown in figure 3, which portrays several of the outstanding *bhikkhunīs* and identifies them by name.

Figure 3. Eminent *bhikkhunī*s, Sulamani gu hpaya, Pagan.

The passages surveyed above put into perspective the misogynist voices surveyed earlier. They also provide a background to the account of the founding of the *bhikkhunī* order, making it clear that this was a positive event and not the onset of some form of decline. The different versions of this account share an explicit affirmation that women can reach all four levels of awakening. In view of this potential, it would be natural for the Buddha to start an order of *bhikkhunī*s and thereby grant women what in the ancient setting were considered to be the ideal conditions for progress to awakening.

The affirmation of women's potential to reach full awakening recurs in the context of a comparison of various qualities required for progress to liberation with parts of a vehicle (*yāna*). The relevant discourse concludes that someone who has such a vehicle, independent of being a woman or a man, will progress to the final goal (translated by Bodhi 2000: 122; the original mentions "a woman" first and only after that "a man"). Whereas the idea of a vehicle continues with the traditions of the Great Vehicle, the Mahāyāna, the soteriological inclusiveness voiced in this discourse has not necessarily been maintained. In the words of Harrison (1987: 78):

> Compared with the situation in the Pāli Canon, in which women are at least as capable as men of attaining the highest goal, arhatship, the position of women in the Mahāyāna has hardly changed for the better, since women cannot attain buddhahood, and even the title of *bodhisattva* is withheld from them. Of course all this reflects the attitudes of the men (probably monks) who produced these texts, but this does

not make the conclusion any less inescapable: although both men and women can ride in the Great Vehicle, only men are allowed to drive it.

In the remainder of this chapter I survey developments that appear to have contributed to this state of affairs.

13. THE BUDDHA AS A MALE

The Buddha himself was of course a male and one of his auspicious bodily marks relates precisely to his genitals. The term used in this context is obscure but can be interpreted by recourse to a simile that regularly accompanies descriptions of this particular mark (Anālayo 2017a: 131–33). The simile compares this mark to a horse.

The male organ of a horse is retractable; in fact, for the general observer it can be quite difficult to differentiate a male from a female horse unless the former is sexually aroused. Since the idea of a retractable male organ would also fit the obscure term used in the discourses, it seems fair to assume that the idea was that the Buddha could retract his male organ. Such would have been an appropriate expression of his complete chastity due to having fully awakened. The discourses regularly report that brahmins trained in the lore of these auspicious bodily marks are able to discern most of them, but with this one they require the Buddha's cooperation. The ability to retract the male organ would indeed require an act of demonstration.

In line with the proposed interpretation of this mark, the standard listing of the other auspicious marks conveys a sense of androgyny. Whereas a comparison of the Buddha's torso and teeth to a lion express a sense of masculinity, the description of the softness of his hands and feet, together with comparisons of his legs to those of an antelope, his eyelashes to those of a cow, and his voice to that of a cuckoo are decidedly not masculine (Anālayo 2017a: 133).

This changes in later times, when the Buddha came to be increasingly cast in the role of a male hero. In particular in some hagiographic accounts of his experiences in youth before going forth, he features as a paragon of masculinity and male prowess. This involves a shift away from how the Buddha is depicted in the early discourses. To some extent, the tendency in later texts to cast the Buddha in the role of a masculine hero could be viewed as the other side of the coin of the attitudes evident in the prediction of decline and similar passages: namely the need to placate male anxiety.

14. ONLY MALES BECOME BUDDHAS

The maleness of the Buddha is of relevance to a Pāli discourse listing five impossibilities for women (translated by Ñāṇamoli 1995/2005: 929). According to this listing, a woman cannot occupy a leading position as a celestial being by serving as a Māra, a Sakka, or a Brahmā, and in the human realm she also cannot be a monarch ruling over the whole earth or a Buddha. A comparative study of the relevant Pāli discourse in the light of its parallels extant from other transmission lineages makes it safe to conclude that this listing is a later addition (Anālayo 2012b: 249–88).

In a patriarchal society like ancient India, a monarch ruling over the whole earth would naturally have been visualized as male. The same reasoning appears to inform the other two heavenly ruling positions, and from there appears to have been applied to Māra as well. The inability to be a Māra could even be considered complimentary rather than discriminatory.

In the early discourses, the Buddha features as a king of Dharma. Moreover, according to a prediction, had he not gone forth he would have become a monarch ruling over the whole earth. From this viewpoint, it is not surprising if a listing of various type of kings also comes to include the Buddha, simply due to being an alternative open to someone who could otherwise become a world monarch.

Moreover, in the patriarchal setting of ancient India a female Buddha would probably not have been taken seriously. The same logic applies to caste, in that Buddhas will be from the higher castes of brahmins or warriors (Anālayo 2012b: 280). It would have been considerably more difficult for a Buddha from a low caste to be respected sufficiently to be able to teach others effectively.

At the same time, the discourses clearly show the Buddha repeatedly dismissing claims to caste superiority, and the Buddhist monastic order was open to members from all castes. In the same vein, the idea that a Buddha is male need not from the outset have been expressive of an inherent superiority of maleness but might just have been due to taking into account hierarchies in ancient India. Moreover, the impossibility at issue is about *being* a Buddha, not about becoming one in a future life. It does not imply an assessment of spiritual ability but only reflects leadership conceptions prevalent in the cultural setting.

The situation changes, however, with an additional impossibility mentioned in some versions of the discourse in question. This is the assertion that a woman cannot be a Paccekabuddha, one who awakens without a teacher but, unlike a Buddha, does not take on the role of teaching others. Since a Paccekabuddha does not teach and is not comparable to a king, leadership requirements are no longer relevant. In this way, the stage is set for associating maleness with superior spiritual abilities.

15. The Buddha's Past Lives as a Male

The Buddha's maleness also influenced ideas related to progress on the path to Buddhahood over several lives, a topic that I will explore in more detail in the next chapter (see p. 46). The idea of such gradual progress to becoming a Buddha naturally stimulated an interest in the Buddha's past lives. These are recorded in *jātaka* tales.

Such *jātaka* tales appear to have originated from similes, anecdotes, and fables taken from ancient Indian narrative lore. The basic reasoning appears to have been that when the Buddha related some such stories, especially if he did so without an explicit indication that he had heard them from someone else, then this should be considered something he had experienced himself in a past life (Anālayo 2010b: 68). As a result, stories originally probably intended as allegories came to be read literally as accounts of something that actually happened. Moreover, the door was open to including various tales of popular appeal among the continuously growing repertoire of the Buddha's accounts of his past lives.

The famous Indian epic *Rāmāyana* is one such tale, with Rāma then identified as a past life of the Buddha (Anālayo 2010b: 58). Another illustrative case is the most popular *jātaka* in the Theravāda tradition, a former life of the Buddha as a prince named Vessantara. The prince gives away everything he has to brahmins, including his wife and children. The difficulty of reconciling his irresponsible behavior with Buddhist ethics finds explanation in the fact that the tale was apparently based on the adoption of a brahminical trope (Anālayo 2017i: 113–41).

The way *jātaka*s evolve can be illustrated with a discourse in which the Buddha compares the need to avoid a loss of mindfulness to the case of a quail that has been caught by a hawk (translated by Bodhi 2000: 1632). Had the quail not strayed out of its domain, it would not have been caught. This serves to inculcate the importance of remaining established in mindfulness as one's own mental domain in order to avoid being caught by Māra. Whereas in its original context the story is just an illustration, without any pretense of reporting an actual event, in the *Jātaka* collection the same tale becomes an actual event from the past and the quail is consequently identified as a former existence of the Buddha (Anālayo 2010b: 60).

In the course of turning a simile, anecdote, or fable into a *jātaka*, one of its protagonists needs to be identified as a past life of the Buddha. Usually, although not exclusively, this will be someone showing exemplary conduct. In the tale just mentioned the choice is clear: the identification of the past life will settle on the quail and not the hawk.

Given the great variety of characters selected in this way, a trait to connect them would naturally have been maleness (Anālayo 2016a: 413–21). To do so would have been in line with a general notion in the ancient Indian setting that gender remains fairly stable across different lives. In this way, identifying predominantly male figures as past lives of the Buddha would have provided some sense of continuity among otherwise widely differing characters.

Although the great majority of *jātaka*s involve lives of the Buddha as a male, an intriguing exception is a tale of a past life in which he was a princess (Anālayo 2016a: 423–42 and Dhammadinnā 2015: 486–94 and

2018: 68–73). Comparative study of this episode nevertheless shows how the influence of negativity toward women affects the way the princess is portrayed, similar to the narrative strategies of devaluation evident in the report of teachings given to Mahāpajāpatī Gotamī and a group of *bhikkhunīs*, mentioned above. In one of the versions, the supposed impossibilities for women come up explicitly. Their mention then motivates the woman (in this version she is not even a princess) to commit suicide in order to get rid of her female body. Although the Buddha of that time intervenes to save her life, her attempt to kill herself still has the desired result, as she is magically transformed into a male (Anālayo 2016a: 436).

The values promoted in this episode accord with a general tendency in later texts to consider birth as a female to be the result of bad karma. Such evaluations are not found in the early texts (Anālayo 2016a: 381–90). This holds even for an early Buddhist cosmogenic myth, according to which the evolution of humans from a previous superior condition is not the result of female temptation but is rather occasioned by the greedy disposition of originally sexless beings (translated by Walshe 1987: 410). The myth does not postulate an inherent superiority of males over females or construe some primordial blame placed on women for the downfall from a paradisiac condition (Anālayo 2019l: 34).

Once the idea of progress to Buddhahood over a series of past lives had arisen, however, the nearly consistent maleness of such past lives of the Buddha must have naturally led to the notion that someone embarking on the path to Buddhahood had better be male at least for the final lives spent progressing to this goal. Although some textual sources show that this was a contested notion (Dhammadinnā 2015/2016 and 2018: 83–86), it nevertheless came to feature as a normative position in both Mahāyāna and Theravāda texts. The relevant texts agree in asserting that women need to be reborn as males in order to be able to progress through the higher stages of the path to becoming a Buddha (Anālayo 2016a: 422).

Summary

The *bhikkhunī* ordination lineage was transmitted from India to Sri Lanka and from there to China, although the latter transmission appears to have happened in a way that does not fully satisfy strict Theravāda legal requirements. Due to the subsequent decline of the order of *bhikkhunīs* in India and Sri Lanka, since the time of the eleventh century there appear to have been no more *bhikkhunīs* ordained according to Theravāda law who could have collaborated with a Theravāda order of *bhikkhus* in granting ordination to a female candidate. Since that time, women wanting to dedicate themselves to a monastic type of life in the Theravāda traditions have faced various forms of discrimination. In the traditional setting, until recently they could only take ordination as eight- or ten-precept nuns, which places them in an ambiguous situation in between the monastic and the lay world.

Monastic law does not envisage the possibility that members of one particular monastic tradition grant valid ordination to members of another monastic tradition. This holds regardless of whether the person to be ordained is male or female. Nevertheless, a solution to the legal problem of reviving an order of *bhikkhunīs* emerges through a close inspection of the relevant parts of the monastic code. When no order of *bhikkhunīs* is in existence, it appears possible for an order of *bhikkhus* to grant ordination to female candidates as a way of reviving an order of *bhikkhunīs* who then can collaborate with the *bhikkhus* in future ordinations.

A key factor influencing the situation of monastic women in the Buddhist traditions is the prediction of decline that according to the *Vinaya* the Buddha supposedly made after establishing an order of *bhikkhunīs*. This prediction of decline, which has failed to come to pass, stands in direct contrast to a range of other passages. It may have gradually originated in the context of retellings of the narrative of a communal recitation held after the Buddha's death.

Comparative study provides a background to the report that the Buddha originally refused to start an order of *bhikkhunīs*. In several accounts of this episode, he grants women the right to shave their heads and wear robes, but apparently also wants them to stay in the protected environment of their homes. This would reflect an apprehension that, at such an early time in the development of the monastic community, it was potentially dangerous for them to live as wandering mendicants in a setting where women unprotected by their family members were vulnerable to abuse. Accounts of the founding of the order of *bhikkhunīs* that do not report the Buddha permitting Mahāpajāpatī and her followers to shave their heads and wear robes still give the impression that some such permission stands behind their narrative progression.

Read on their own, however, such accounts evoke a negative impression of the Buddha's attitude, as he seems just unwilling to start an order of *bhikkhunīs* at all. Such negative impressions are in line with narrative strategies of devaluation of women that can be identified elsewhere in individual texts, some of which reflect the influence of ancient Indian voices of misogyny impacting the Buddhist tradition already at quite an early time. These stand in contrast to a range of passages presenting a positive appraisal of women and their potential, among others attesting to a clear recognition of their ability to reach all of the four stages of awakening.

Depictions of the Buddha in the early texts do not present him as a paragon of masculinity, unlike later texts. According to a listing of impossibilities, a woman cannot be a Buddha. Although probably originating from leadership conceptions in the ancient Indian setting, where a female stood little chance of being recognized as an accomplished teacher, the idea of such an impossibility could easily have fostered a tendency to belittle women's abilities. This had an impact in particular on conceptions of the path to Buddhahood, in that the accomplishment of an advanced bodhisattva came eventually to be seen as manifesting in the leaving behind of the female body in order to continue for the rest of *his* career as a male.

The various strands of negativity toward women that emerge in this way are not in conformity with the early teachings. After the Buddha's passing away, it was perhaps natural for ensuing generations of Buddhist monastics to move more in line with general biases prevalent in the patriarchal setting of ancient India, in their attempt to ensure the survival of the fledgling tradition in the face of competition with other religious groups and under the threat of internal disintegration.

Thanks to the efforts of the Buddhist monastic institutions over many centuries the teachings and discipline have been transmitted until today.

Without in any way intending to turn a blind eye to this remarkable achievement of past generations, it nevertheless needs to be recognized that to insist on perpetuating outdated hierarchies based on male superiority conceit is not in keeping with the demands of current times and is detrimental to the welfare of the Buddhist traditions it seeks to protect.

II. Mahāyāna Buddhism

INTRODUCTION

MY EXPLORATION IN this chapter concerns a form of superiority conceit found among some Mahāyāna Buddhists. This finds expression in the belief that membership in the Great Vehicle, the Mahāyāna, automatically confers superiority over anyone else who does not aspire to Buddhahood. This assumption can at times lead to various modes of denigration, such as the employment of Hīnayāna rhetoric. In order to show that the underlying sense of superiority lacks a historical foundation, I study in particular textual evidence for the gradual arising of the bodhisattva ideal, a topic to which most of the present chapter is dedicated. Needless to say, such textual evidence can provide only a limited reflection of what must have been complex and multidimensional developments. Nevertheless, the early discourses do provide hints at what must have been key aspects of these developments.

As a starting point, I take up the Buddha's auspicious bodily marks, a topic already broached in the last chapter. This leads me to the theme of past and future Buddhas and the role of compassion in the historical Buddha's motivation to pursue awakening. Then I examine later conceptions of compassion and the idea of self-sacrifice, in particular the trope of intentionally setting oneself on fire.

A sense of intrinsic superiority among those pursuing the path of a bodhisattva appears to have provided a fertile environment for the appeal of the idea that the mind is similarly intrinsically superior, in the sense of being by nature pure and luminous. A particularly blatant expression of the sense of superiority is the use of Hīnayāna rhetoric, which turns out to originate from the polemical need to authenticate Mahāyāna scriptures, in the sense of asserting that these texts originated with the historical Buddha. Hīnayāna rhetoric has its counterpart in eulogizing the heroism of bodhisattvas; in fact, the same tendency to claim superiority can even lead to condescending attitudes toward other Mahāyāna practitioners.

1. THE CONCEPTION OF THE BUDDHA'S MARKS

The Buddha's auspicious bodily marks already came up in the last chapter (see p. 32), in particular the nature of his male organ and its relation to the idea that only males can become a Buddha or even be on the higher stages of progress of the path to Buddhahood. The early texts report that right away at birth these marks can serve as portents of the eventual attainment of Buddhahood by the person endowed with them (translated by Bodhi 2017: 275). In what follows, I explore their general significance and role.

As mentioned in the previous chapter, the terminology used to describe the Buddha's male organ is somewhat obscure, although the accompanying simile gives the impression that the idea would have been that he was able to retract it. Another bodily mark of the Buddha, whose description is in contrast quite clear, takes the form of a wheel on the soles of his feet. This wheel mark portends his destiny that, after having gone forth and reached awakening, he will eventually be surrounded by many disciples from all of the four assemblies. An issue with this mark is how literally the idea of a wheel on the soles of his feet should be taken.

This topic comes up in a discourse reporting that a brahmin had seen a footprint of the Buddha (translated by Bodhi 2012: 425). The parallel versions differ in their depiction of this footprint (Anālayo 2017a: 14–26). One version just has a bare footprint, in several others the footprint has the mark of a wheel, and in one version this wheel is brilliant and resplendent.

For the Buddha's feet to be able to leave the imprint of a wheel mark on the ground, the wheels on the soles of his feet must have at least some degree of hardness and elevation, otherwise they could not result in visible tracks on the soil. Such a literal understanding, however, stands in contrast to another of the auspicious bodily marks of the Buddha, which describes the softness of his feet and hands (translated by Ñāṇamoli 1995/2005: 745). Moreover, it would also not be easy to understand why only this discourse reports that his feet left such noticeable imprints. Had they been endowed with such ability to affect the ground over which the Buddha had walked, one would expect to find this remarkable effect being mentioned more often.

Another instance, in a comparatively early Pāli commentary that also involves the Buddha's footprint, does not have any reference to a wheel mark (translated by Bodhi 2017: 1106). Here the idea is simply that the way of walking can reflect the overall temperament of the walker. Someone who has sensual desire will drag the feet, one with anger will contract the toes, and one under the influence of delusion will trample on the ground. On close examination of someone's footprint, a keen observer could detect traces of these distinct modes of walking and then draw conclusions regarding the mental propensities of the walker. The same idea could also have been in the background of the above-mentioned instance involving the brahmin who had seen a footprint of the Buddha. In this case, the idea of an actual imprint of a wheel mark in the footprint, rather than just a bare footprint, would be a later development (Anālayo 2017a: 29).

Such a conclusion would be in line with a tendency evident in other marks of the Buddha. A particularly striking example is the idea that he had some sort of protuberance on his head (Anālayo 2017a: 51–54). This appears to have originated in a tendency in ancient Indian art to portray gods and spiritual teachers with long hair, often worn in a topknot. The same custom was employed even in the portrayal of Jain saints, despite the fact that, in following Jain customs, they must have plucked out their hair on going forth.

In the case of the Buddha, there is considerable textual evidence that he was shaven-headed instead of having long hair worn in a topknot, and also that he was not easily distinguishable from some of his disciples (Anālayo 2017a: 57–61). Relevant episodes involve encounters with a king, the guardian of a park, and a Buddhist monastic who was meeting the Buddha for the first time. Their failure to recognize him implies that, from the viewpoint of the textual reports of these encounters, he was not considered to have had some sort of cranial protuberance or any other unusual bodily feature that would have made it easy for others to identify him.

The way these marks have come down in tradition appears to be the

Figure 4. Worshipping the Buddha's footprints,
adorned with wheel marks; Amarāvatī.

result of some degree of cross-fertilization between text and art, where
a certain idea is concretized in pictorial presentation and this in turn
leads to a further fleshing out of textual descriptions. Due to such cross-
fertilization, it is not easy to make sense of the descriptions of these marks
in the way they are now found in the texts. A literal reading of such
descriptions would in fact invest the Buddha with a bodily appearance
quite easily recognized, due to highly unusual physical features.

Similarly, in the case of the wheel mark the original idea of this physical
feature might have stood for something not immediately visible, be this
on the soles of the feet or on the ground. During an early period of Indian
art, there seems to have been a preference not to depict the Buddha himself and instead to allude to his presence symbolically, a tendency often
referred to as "aniconism." An obvious choice for such an aniconic form
of depiction must have been the Buddha's footprints. In order to indicate that these were the footprints left by the one who had set in motion
the wheel of Dharma—this being the title of the Buddha's famous first
discourse—wheel marks on these feet are an obvious choice. Such footprints, adorned with wheel marks, could have conveniently functioned as
an object of worship. Besides being easily identifiable as representing the

Buddha, they would also have enabled an emulation of the way worship was expressed by those who actually met the Buddha, namely by paying respect at his feet. Such worship of the Buddha's footprint can be seen in the sculpture shown in figure 4.

2. THE ROLE OF THE BUDDHA'S MARKS

Several early discourses refer to the ability to recognize the Buddha's auspicious bodily marks as the special province of brahmins (Anālayo 2017a: 61–68). The requirement to have trained in the lore of these marks confirms that originally a recognition of these bodily features was considered to be beyond the ken of the average observer not proficient in the art of discerning them. In other words, however hyperbolically they eventually came to be described, originally these marks must have been about rather subtle nuances.

Their depiction could be compared to referring to a human body as being "in the bloom of youth." This does not imply that the person in question is growing petals; the motif of a blooming flower has only a metaphorical sense. Now suppose someone decides to illustrate this with the help of a drawing that shows actual petals. If on seeing such a drawing someone else were then to take the illustration literally, the result would be the idea of a human being with actual petals. Depictions of the Buddha's bodily marks seem to have followed a comparable trajectory.

With the passage of time, the marks also acquired a more general function of conversion, beyond the restricted range of brahmins trained in their lore (Anālayo 2017a: 94–101), as a result of which the marks inevitably came to be conceived as more readily visible. Such a development aligns with the tendency, mentioned above, for the depiction of these marks to evolve in an ongoing dialogue between texts and art.

A rather specific role of the marks emerges in a Pāli discourse that relates each of these to particular qualities or endowments of the Buddha (Anālayo 2017a: 103–35). The discourse begins with the premise that, even though non-Buddhists are also aware of these auspicious marks, they do not know what particular karmic deed led to which mark (translated by Walshe 1987: 442). In this discourse, the lore of the bodily marks is placed firmly within the scope of the early Buddhist doctrine of causality by relating a particular mark to a specific type of conduct adopted in the past.

The exposition in this Pāli discourse, absent from its parallel and undoubtedly reflecting a later development, goes into great detail to explain precisely what type of action undertaken in a former lifetime led to the Buddha now having a particular mark. In the case of the wheel mark, for example, protecting others and ensuring their happiness during previous lives should be seen as the relevant karmic deeds undertaken in former times. These are responsible for the manifestation of such a mark on the soles of the Buddha's feet in his present life.

The idea of relating the marks to conditionality as such is in line with a pervasive concern with karma and causality in early Buddhist thought. The resultant presentation, however, conveys the idea that a specific type of conduct during a series of past lives is required in order to become a Buddha. This idea, which is otherwise not attested among the early discourses, is of considerable importance for the gradual evolution of the bodhisattva ideal.

3. Past and Future Buddhas

The well-known motif of the future Buddha Gotama's aspiration to Buddhahood, on the occasion of meeting the previous Buddha Dīpaṃkara, is absent from the early discourses. According to Nattier (2004: 230), the lack of any reference to this meeting among the early discourses "makes it virtually certain that traditions concerning this buddha did not gain general currency until several centuries after Śākyamuni Buddha's death." The early discourses know only six former Buddhas, the first of which is Vipassin and the last Kassapa. Figure 5 shows the seven Buddhas, with the present Buddha as the main figure and the six former Buddhas depicted below him.

A detailed textual description of the Buddha Vipassin covers also his auspicious bodily marks (translated by Walshe 1987: 205). Closer inspection brings to light that, at an early stage in the evolution of these descrip-

Figure 5. The Buddha (depicted with a topknot)
and his six predecessors below; Gandhāra.

tions, the marks were apparently not yet considered an invariable feature of all Buddhas (Anālayo 2017a: 87–89). In other words, although one who is endowed with these marks and goes forth will become a Buddha, possession of the marks was not from the outset seen as an indispensable requirement for Buddhahood. By way of illustration, although a crown prince can be expected to become king, being a crown prince is not an indispensable requirement for assuming the throne; at times someone may be crowned ruler who is not even a descendant of the previous king, let alone the crown prince.

In addition to these six predecessors, Maitreya as a future Buddha features in one Pāli discourse (translated by Walshe 1987: 403). Comparative study of the parallel versions of this discourse makes it highly likely that the idea of the future Buddha Maitreya is a later addition (Anālayo 2010b: 95–113 and 2017b: 383–91). The discourse in question appears to have originated from the delivery of a parable that illustrates the dire repercussions of immoral behavior by depicting a general decline in living conditions, in contrast to moral behavior and its consequences. Collins (1998: 494) remarks that

> it may seem odd, indeed unacceptable, to the dour-faced and humorless positivism with which these texts are so often read . . . that the earliest text-place where a reference to the future Buddha is found should be a humorous parable whose main burden is to relativize and diminish all temporal goods, past, present and future.

For the teaching conveyed in this parable to function, a reference to Maitreya is not required. This can be seen quite well in one of the three extant versions, which does not mention the future Buddha Maitreya at all. His appearance in the other two discourses appears to be the result of an embellishment of the parable, which in all versions leads up to the depiction of a king who peacefully rules over the whole earth. This forms the culmination point of a general improvement of living conditions due to moral conduct.

In line with a recurrent trope, the ruler of the world eventually decides to renounce and go forth. Presumably as a way of improving on the effect created in this way, in two of the three versions he becomes an arahant. In order to do so, however, he would need a Buddha to give him the teachings required for progress to awakening. This may have been the motivation for the introduction of a future Buddha into the story (Anālayo 2017b: 385).

The resultant detailed description of the actions taken in the distant future by the king and the Buddha Maitreya does not conform

to the early Buddhist notion of causality (Anālayo 2010b: 108). To be able to predict with certainty the names and actions of individuals in the distant future requires a form of predeterminism, leaving no room for those involved to make individual decisions resulting in a course of action different from the one predicted. The present case is the only instance in the early discourses where such a detailed prediction of the distant future occurs. According to the early Buddhist notion of causality, events are the result of a complex interplay of various causes and conditions, among which individual decisions play their role. This prevents predicting with complete certainty the type of details in a distant future time in the way this is the case in the depiction of the advent of Maitreya.

4. Maitreya and Kassapa Buddha

A reference to Maitreya's advent also occurs in another discourse, extant in Chinese, where closer inspection similarly shows this element to be also a later addition (Anālayo 2010b: 113–18). The additional part reports that two monastics aspire to be reborn as the king and the Buddha of that future time. The Buddha rebukes the monastic who aspires to become the ruler of the world and commends the one who wishes to become the future Buddha Maitreya; he then predicts that both will succeed in their aspirations.

A precedent to this type of prediction can be found in depictions of brahmins whose skill in the lore of auspicious bodily marks enabled them to ascertain whether an infant had the potential to become a Buddha or a monarch reigning over the whole world (Anālayo 2017a: 86–87). A difference here is that the predictions given by such brahmins concern a potential to be realized in the same life; they do not predict what will happen in another life in the distant future.

Closer study of the aspirations of the two monastics and the Buddha's reply shows a pattern of textual repetition, as a result of which the description of the beatific conditions of that future time are repeated as many as eight times (Anālayo 2010b: 118–28). Although repetition is a regular feature of the early discourses, the degree to which this occurs in this case is remarkable. Given the relatively late nature of the relevant part of the discourse, it must have originated at some time after the Buddha had passed away and hence in a situation where the loss of his leadership must have been acutely felt among the faithful. The purpose of the text could well have been to reassure the audience, by dint of repeated affirmation, of the advent of another Buddha in the future. In this way, the motif of the coming Buddha Maitreya conveys a sense of fearlessness, a feature also evident in the sculpture shown in figure 6.

The circumstance that two of these eight repetitions take the form of a prediction that the two monastics will become the ruler of the world and the Buddha respectively appears to be more a by-product of this main purpose of conveying a sense of reassurance. Once the idea of predicting someone's future Buddhahood had arisen, be it in this episode or in some other context, it does not take much to apply the same to the Buddha Gotama.

A passage reflecting a closely related notion occurs in yet another discourse, whose main concern is to extol the Buddha. The relevant part lists one of his marvelous qualities. Mentioned in a Chinese version of this discourse but absent from the Pāli parallel, this particular quality is indubitably a later addition. The marvelous quality in question is his original vow to become a Buddha, a vow attributed to a past life of his as a monastic disciple of the previous Buddha Kassapa (Anālayo 2010b: 84–92). In this way, whereas the type of aspiration made by one of the two monastics in the other episode surveyed above happens in the present and concerns the future Buddha Maitreya, in this episode the same type of aspiration occurred in the past and stands in the background of the advent of the present Buddha Gotama.

The circumstance that this aspiration is considered a marvel in its own right makes it fair to assume that this description came into existence when the idea of such aspirations to Buddhahood was not yet well established, otherwise it would not have stood much chance of being considered an outstanding and marvelous quality. A meeting with

Figure 6. The Bodhisattva Maitreya, his right hand in the gesture
of fearlessness, with a small wheel incised in his palm; Mathurā.

the previous Buddha indeed provides a natural catalyst for the idea of
aspiring to become a Buddha oneself. With the passage of time and the
increasing glorification of the Buddha, the period required for cultivating the necessary qualifications for Buddhahood must have gradually
expanded. As a result, his original aspiration would have shifted further
into the past, until it came to be associated with a former life at the time
of the Buddha Dīpaṅkara.

5. THE BUDDHA GOTAMA'S MOTIVATION

The early discourses conceive of the Buddha's progress to awakening entirely from within the framework of his present life, rather than presenting it as a trajectory spanning over a series of former lives spent under the overarching intention to become a Buddha in the future. In the same texts, the term *bodhisattva* does not yet carry connotations of a prolonged preparation for Buddhahood over many lifetimes. Instead, at this stage in the development of Buddhist thought it predominantly designates the period in the Buddha's present life when he had set out in quest of awakening (Anālayo 2010b: 15–19).

The perfections (*pāramitā*), a set of qualities considered by later tradition to be required for progress to Buddhahood, are not even mentioned in the Pāli discourses or in their parallels. The early discourses rather depict the future Buddha's progress to awakening in ways similar to standard accounts of how to become an arahant. This concords with a general principle, according to which the Buddha taught others what he practiced himself and in turn practiced himself what he taught to others (translated by Bodhi 2012: 410). According to the same texts, in their spiritual quest the Buddha's disciples can emulate other accomplished disciples (Anālayo 2010b: 53); that is, they need not take only the Buddha himself as their role model.

Accounts of what motivated the Buddha-to-be to embark on the quest for awakening convey that his aim was to liberate himself rather than the wish to liberate others (Anālayo 2010b: 20–26). The same holds for the report of his successful completion of his quest, whereby he had achieved liberation from the prospect of future rebirth. The relevant passage does not have a reference to being able to save others (translated by Ñāṇamoli 1995/2005: 259). In this way, from his initial motivation to his successful completion of his quest, the texts show the Buddha's predominant concern to be with himself. As noted by Wangchuk (2007: 82)

> there is no canonical evidence for the theory that the main motive for the Buddha's appearance in the world was for the sake of others. This idea is found only in the post-canonical

literature. The overwhelming majority of the canonical material suggests that the Buddha's renunciation of worldly life and his search for salvation from *saṃsāra* were exclusively or primarily motivated by the realisation that he himself was inevitably affected by aging, sickness, and death, and that he was concerned with his own release (*vimukti*). Once he had attained his own release from *saṃsāra*, he could have, if he wanted, retreated and acted like a 'solitary awakened one' (*pratyekabuddha*), that is, without propagating his teaching systematically.

This does not mean that the Buddha was bereft of compassion. It does mean, however, that his compassion was not seen as substantially different from that of his fully awakened disciples (Anālayo 2010b: 26–27). In both cases, compassion results from having reached awakening and thereby having eradicated the type of mental defilements that could obstruct compassion. The motivation leading to such awakening, however, is the wish to be liberated oneself rather than the aspiration to save others.

In sum, with the passages surveyed above the gradual emergence of central aspects of the bodhisattva ideal can be discerned. Beyond any doubt, this ideal was something as yet unknown at the time of the historical Buddha and the first generations of his disciples.

6. Changing Conceptions of Compassion

The lack of a prominent role for compassion in the conception of the motivation to set out on the quest for Buddhahood continues beyond the early discourses to texts that reflect early stages of Mahāyāna thought (Anālayo 2010b: 28). With the passage of time, however, compassion became a central dimension of the bodhisattva path. In this setting, it came to fulfill the role of supporting a bodhisattva's motivation. Several texts highlight the aspiration of bodhisattvas to lead others to liberation before attaining the same themselves (Anālayo 2017d: 99–101). A related theme in this type of texts is the idea of being willing to take unto oneself the suffering of all living beings, even to the extent of being ready to be reborn in hell just for the sake of delivering sentient beings. At times such attitudes are juxtaposed with the inferior compassion of those who do not follow the path to Buddhahood, due to their fear of suffering. In contrast, the compassionate bodhisattva remains fearless in the face of any suffering and is willing to postpone entry into Nirvana until all other sentient beings have been saved.

The fearless willingness to take unto oneself the suffering of all living beings differs from compassion in early Buddhist thought, which can serve as a means of gaining deep concentration. For this purpose, the actual experience of compassion needs to be conjoined with a pleasant hedonic tone, thereby being productive of joy. This would be difficult to achieve once the pain of another is taken onto oneself.

The cultivation of compassion described in the early texts does not focus on the pain of others, but much rather takes as its object the aspiration that others become free from whatever affliction they may have. Due to taking this perspective, a keen apperception of actual instances of suffering can lead over to a mental state free from pain, achieved by attending to the potential of release from that suffering. Having cultivated such a mental attitude then finds its practical expression in undertaking what is needed to enable others to achieve freedom from the causes of their affliction and distress.

The main thrust of the early Buddhist conception of compassion could be summarized as the wish for the absence of harm, be this harm inflicted by oneself, by others, or just by adverse circumstances (Anālayo 2017d: 89). Here compassion stands in the context of a set of four commendable mental attitudes (Anālayo 2015a: 28–49). These are reckoned to be "divine abodes" (*brahmavihāra*), an expression that can be taken to convey that these mental dispositions are more heavenly than worldly. Alternatively, these four are also referred to as "boundless states;" in fact, they quite literally transcend the bounds of self-centeredness, and their cultivation involves an unlimited radiation in all directions (Anālayo 2019d).

The first of these four sublime mental attitudes, loving kindness or benevolence (*mettā*), is the one most often mentioned in the early discourses. Building on the foundation laid by kind and benevolent conduct and attitude, compassion then falls into place, leading to sympathetic joy and equanimity. The four divine abodes taken together offer ways of responding with an open heart to whatever situation or challenge may present itself. In other words, here compassion is not the default attitude invariably to be adopted, as at times one of the other three divine abodes could be more appropriate. On occasions it might be preferable to opt for equanimity, for example.

The path of practice in early Buddhist thought comprises training in morality, concentration, and wisdom. Compassion relates to each of these three trainings (Anālayo 2017d: 88–89). The first of the five precepts to be observed by any disciple of the Buddha requires abstention from killing living beings, the standard description of which explicitly reckons such abstention to be an expression of compassion. As already mentioned, the meditative cultivation of compassion can function as a powerful entry into deep states of mental tranquility. The compassionate intention for the absence of harm is one of the three right intentions, the second factor of the noble eightfold path. Together with right view, right intention belongs to the division of wisdom of this noble eightfold path. In this way, the relation of compassion to morality, concentration, and wisdom shows its ubiquitous role in the early Buddhist conception of the path to awakening, even though this does not involve the willingness to take unto oneself the suffering of other or even all living beings.

7. Burning for the Buddha

The rhetoric of self-sacrifice for the sake of others, extolled as the acme of compassion in some later texts, can at times inspire rather drastic enactments. A prominent example is the act of self-immolation. Here, too, comparative study can provide hints at the possible origins of such a practice.

A relevant episode among the early discourses describes a monastic who requests the Buddha's permission to enter into final Nirvana. The permission received, the monastic magically rises up into space and miraculously cremates himself (translated by Ireland 1990: 124). Closer inspection of the parallel versions of this episode makes it possible that this prose description originated from a literal reading of a verse that illustrates an arahant's freedom from future rebirth with the example of a burning spark that becomes extinguished (Anālayo 2015d: 389–414). In other words, the original idea need not have been some form of self-cremation.

In texts on monastic discipline, the same monastic features as an adept in meditation on the fire element, which enabled him to set his finger on fire in order to illuminate the walking paths for other monastics who had arrived at the monastery late at night. The depiction of his supernormal ability in this respect, also evident in his capability to perform a self-cremation, is the only such instance shared by parallel versions of the respective texts.

Descriptions of this monastic's mastery over the fire element appear to have in turn influenced later texts that describe bodhisattvas who set either their whole body or parts of it on fire. Already in themselves quite probably the result of literalism, such descriptions have in turn become scripts acted out by practicing Buddhists. In particular one such episode in the Lotus Sūtra has inspired acts of actual self-immolation, at times accompanied by a recitation of the passage in question (Benn 2007). Subsequent texts sanction such acts, to the extent of proclaiming that to be reckoned a bodhisattva who has gone forth requires burning one's body, an arm, or a finger as an offering for Buddhas (Anālayo 2015d: 401n41). In this way, a poetic spark may have set human fires burning through the history of Buddhism up to modern times.

8. The Superiority of Bodhisattvas

The fearless willingness to take unto oneself the suffering of others, even being willing to set oneself on fire as an offering for Buddhas, stands in line with a general trend of attributing superiority to bodhisattvas. Similar to other elements surveyed above, the basic notion of such superiority has a precedent in a passage in the early discourses.

The relevant passage occurs in the Pāli version of the discourse on the marvelous qualities of the Buddha (translated by Ñāṇamoli 1995/2005: 983). Whereas this Pāli version does not mention his initial vow to become a Buddha in the future, it does report a momentous declaration made by him right after being born (translated below). The absence of this declaration in the parallel makes it safe to consider this to be another later addition, just like the reference to the original vow to pursue Buddhahood.

The tendency toward addition in the Pāli version can be seen particularly well in relation to another marvel, also absent from its parallel. This marvel is the passing away of the Buddha's mother seven days after he was born (Anālayo 2010b: 32–33). The mention of this fact occurs in an otherwise chronological listing of marvels. Departing from this sequence, the description of the mother's passing away stands before the depiction of his birth, although her death of course occurred only after his birth. In addition to this sequential problem, the premature decease of the mother also does not naturally fit the idea of a marvelous quality of the future Buddha himself. This makes it fair to conclude that a reference to the mother's early death was added to the discourse during oral transmission, perhaps taken over from another discourse mentioning her premature passing away.

In line with this tendency toward accretion, a textual element found only in the Pāli version is the momentous declaration, made by the future Buddha right after his birth (Anālayo 2010b: 39):

> I am supreme in the world, I am the highest in the world, I am the first in the world; this is my last birth, there will be no further existence.

In this case, the marvelous nature of this proclamation appears to lie in particular in the content of what was said, as elsewhere the discourses report another infant also able to speak right at birth (translated by Walshe 1987: 115). Yet, this ability is not reckoned as being particularly marvelous (Anālayo 2010b: 39–41).

The future Buddha's proclamation itself could be another instance where a textual piece from a different discourse made its way into the present one during oral transmission. As part of an overall tendency to glorify the Buddha, it would hardly be surprising if his transcendence of future rebirth and his resultant superiority over others by dint of having reached full awakening were to find mention. Since the Pāli discourse lists qualities concerned with what preceded and what accompanied the future Buddha's birth, the addition of such a declaration becomes naturally associated with the time of just being born.

The attribution of this proclamation to the time immediately following the future Buddha's birth, however, results in investing the infant with qualities he attained only after having grown up and reached full awakening (Anālayo 2010b: 42–46). At the time of his birth, he was not yet beyond future rebirth, nor could he have claimed to be the foremost of all beings. The account of the future Buddha's course of practice, after going forth, leaves no doubt that he had to struggle with various defilements, in particular sensuality (Anālayo 2010b: 16–19). The roots of these defilements must have been present in his mind at his birth, which in turn implies that at that time he had not yet gone beyond the prospect of future rebirth, nor had he already become the supreme, the highest, and the foremost being in the world.

The tendency to conflate the condition he eventually reached by becoming a Buddha with his infancy is in itself unsurprising. A testimony to the same tendency can be found in an ancient Indian inscription in Lumbini which states that "here the Buddha was born" (Anālayo 2010b: 16n3). The usage of the term "Buddha" to refer to the infant is natural, even though at the time of being born he was of course not yet a Buddha. The coming into being of the future Buddha's proclamation, quoted above, could similarly result from a simple conflation, without awareness of the implications this statement might convey in later times.

The type of proclamation made by the infant Gotama recurs in a description of qualities of his six predecessors, who make the same statement (translated by Walshe 1987: 205). This turns an individual instance into a general pattern (Anālayo 2010b: 50). With a literal reading of this statement, it follows that progress to Buddhahood has already been completed at birth. This ties in with the notion that the actual cultivation required to become a Buddha should be allocated to previous lives. Here the karmic perspective on the Buddha's marks, mentioned earlier in this chapter (see p. 45), falls into place by providing a script for progress to Buddhahood.

Another significant result of the statement quoted above, once this came to be seen as a feat performed by all Buddhas, is that anyone about to become a Buddha in the same life can make such a claim. In other words, worldwide superiority becomes a birth right of bodhisattvas in their last lives. Once such a sense of supremacy has arisen, it does not take much to extend the same to bodhisattvas who are firmly on the path to Buddhahood but have not yet reached their last life. In this way, this type of momentous proclamation attributed to the infant Buddha may have set a precedent for a pervasive sense of superiority among practitioners of the bodhisattva path.

The figure on the cover of this book, which depicts the infant who was to become the Buddha Gotama raising his arm and making this momentous proclamation, encapsulates in a single image the main message. It also reflects various strands of my exploration in the four chapters of this book. The infant is evidently a male. He makes a statement that foreshadows a current in Mahāyāna thought. The probably earliest version of this statement occurs in a discourse transmitted by Theravāda reciters. The statue itself belongs to a Buddhist monastery in the West, where it is regularly used to celebrate the birthday of the Buddha.

9. The Luminous Mind

The idea of being already endowed with the qualities of a fully awakened one at birth would have provided a congenial setting for the arising of the notion of the mind being from the outset already endowed with purity. A trajectory of considerable significance for tracing the arising of this notion emerges from examining a simile that illustrates the gradual purification of the mind with the example of the progressive purification of gold. Comparative study of the relevant early discourses shows that, in the course of oral transmission, qualities originally meant to describe the gold subsequently appear to have been applied to the mind (Anālayo 2017e: 22–26). As a result of what in the course of oral transmission would be quite a natural occurrence, the mind came to be associated with a form of luminosity comparable to the gold mentioned in the simile.

The association of such luminosity with the mind then stands in the background of another passage that contrasts the presence of defilements to their absence. The discourse relates both the presence and the absence of defilements to the luminous condition of the mind (translated by Bodhi 2012: 97). A quotation of this discourse in an Abhidharma work extant in Chinese speaks instead of the condition of the mind as pure (Anālayo 2017e: 26–36).

A problem with the discourse passage in question is its mention of the presence of defilements alongside the qualification of the mind as luminous. Early Buddhist thought recognizes, in line with other spiritual traditions, inner experiences of mental light or inner brightness. However, such experiences require the absence, at least temporarily, of defilements and the cultivation of concentration. The idea that the nature of consciousness as such is to illumine its objects, be this understood literally or metaphorically, appears to be a later development.

The idea that even the defiled mind is luminous is not found elsewhere in early Buddhist thought. It might be the outcome of an insertion of the quality of luminosity into a statement that originally simply contrasted the presence of defilements to their absence. As a result of the apparent introduction of the qualification of being luminous in this context, however, the discourse ends up stating that the mind is luminous even when defilements are present. The trend of replacing "luminous" with "pure," evident in the Abhidharma work just mentioned, could then lead to the idea that the mind is pure even when defiled.

The idea of a luminous and pure nature of the mind that is independent of the presence of defilements has in turn had considerable impact on later texts and practice traditions, leading to the idea that the mind is intrinsically pure and already awakened (Anālayo 2017e: 36–43). From this viewpoint, meditation practice is no longer about gradually removing defilements but much rather requires recognizing this awakened condition as the true nature of the mind.

Inviting an appreciation of this apparent historical development is not meant in any way to deny that practice lineages aimed at experiencing the nature of the mind can yield rather powerful meditative experiences with considerable deconstructive potential. Nor is the subjective experience of inner light during deeper levels of concentration being put into question. The point is only about the notion that the mind is inherently endowed with the superior qualities of purity and luminosity.

Such a notion about the mind's intrinsic superior nature ties in easily with the trajectory of associating the status of a bodhisattva with an intrinsic sense of superiority. Although the assumption of a fundamentally pure nature of the mind can also be found in the Thai tradition of Theravāda Buddhism (Anālayo 2017e: 42–43), the appeal of this notion has been particularly strong among Mahāyāna practice lineages. A central reason could well be its natural resonance with the claim to superiority of advanced bodhisattva practitioners.

10. The Need for Authentication

As mentioned briefly earlier, superiority claims by followers of the Great Vehicle find their most blatant expression in the employment of the term "Hīnayāna." The first part of this term, *hīna*, literally means "inferior," "lowly," "faulty," or "deficient." The English expression "small vehicle" is not a rendering of the Sanskrit term "Hīnayāna" but rather a euphemism used in Chinese translations. The basic idea that stands behind the employment of the term "Hīnayāna" is to provide a contrast to the Mahāyāna, in the sense of juxtaposing those who have not embarked on the bodhisattva path, for this reason being considered inferior, to those who have dedicated themselves to progress to Buddhahood.

The term "Hīnayāna" features, for example, in the biography of Vasubandhu's conversion to the Mahāyāna. According to this biography, at first Vasubandhu had no faith in the Mahāyāna, as he believed this was not taught by the Buddha. After his conversion, however, Vasubandhu offered several arguments to counter the perennial challenge of establishing a direct relationship between the Mahāyāna and the word of the Buddha (Anālayo 2016a: 479–82). Simply stated, the problem underlying this issue is the felt need to authenticate central scriptures considered sacred by attributing them to the historical Buddha. This tendency is pervasive in different Buddhist traditions and is not confined to followers of the Mahāyāna.

One argument to establish a connection between the historical Buddha and the Mahāyāna traditions takes the form of asserting that such teachings were found in a collection of texts that were not part of a communal recitation undertaken by the disciples of the so-called eighteen schools. Being unable to understand Mahāyāna teachings, so the argument goes, the disciples of these eighteen schools had not included them at the first communal recitation, *saṅgīti*, which according to tradition was held soon after the Buddha's death.

Here the expression "schools," *nikāya*s, refers to the different monastic ordination traditions that came into being over the course of time in ancient India. The number "eighteen" in turn is probably best taken in a symbolic sense, in line with a general tendency for numbers being used in this way in ancient Indian literature, rather than being an accurate reflection of historical reality.

Due to not including Mahāyāna teachings in their communal recitation, the eighteen schools came to be designated as Hīnayāna. In this way, the application of the term "Hīnayāna" to the eighteen schools emerges in a polemical context. It serves as an expedient reply to the challenge of lacking canonical authority.

The Chinese pilgrims Faxian, Xuanzang, and Yijing report from their travels in India that they found members of the eighteen schools practicing both Hīnayāna and Mahāyāna (Anālayo 2016a: 474–79). If all eighteen schools belong to the Hīnayāna, it is hardly possible that some of them were practitioners of the Mahāyāna. The two terms "Hīnayāna" and "Mahāyāna" are mutually exclusive. Either one follows the bodhisattva path or one does not.

The solution comes once it is recognized that the distinction between these two alternatives is a vocational one. In contrast, membership in the eighteen schools concerns different monastic ordination traditions. The two distinctions have no necessary relation to each other (Gombrich 1988: 112). Being part of a school in the sense of a monastic ordination tradition comes about through taking ordination. Practicing the bodhisattva path, in contrast, is a vocational decision that has no bearing on whether one takes ordination or not, let alone into which school one ordains. In fact, followers of the Mahāyāna can be found among both monastics and laity.

In this way, the situation the Chinese pilgrims encountered in the homeland of Buddhism clarifies that membership in any of the eighteen schools needs to be differentiated from one's vocation. Some monastics, who must have been members of one of the eighteen schools, did embark on the Mahāyāna. Others did not. This implies that the employment of the term "Hīnayāna" for all the eighteen schools is without a grounding in historical reality.

11. HĪNAYĀNA RHETORIC

Not only is the term "Hīnayāna" not applicable to the eighteen schools, it appears to be entirely a product of imagination. In the words of Silk (2002: 367–68),

> the referent of the term "Hīnayāna," when it occurs in Buddhist texts themselves, is never any existent institution or organization, but a rhetorical fiction . . . a fundamental error is thus made when we imagine references to "Hīnayāna" in Mahāyāna literature to apply to so-called Sectarian Buddhism, much less to Early Buddhism.

In the same vein, Skilling (2013: 76–77) explains:

> There was never, during any period of Indian history, anywhere or at any time, any body of people or any social group—any sect, any faction, any monastic order, or any lay community—which identified itself as 'Hīnayāna.' The Hīnayāna never existed, anywhere or at any time, as an establishment or organization, as a social movement, as a self-conscious historical agent. Nor was Hīnayāna a stage or period in the development of Buddhism. What, then, was the referent of the term? What was its societal reality? Its referent was a body of ideas, not a social body. The Hīnayānist was defined by Mahāyānist polemics; he was a dogmatic construction, not a social identity. He was a straw man, a will-o'-the-wisp . . . Buddhism is a complex entity which has evolved over a vast area for more than two thousand years. To force its development—whether social or historical, whether philosophical or ritual or art-historical—into an

artificial and binary Hīnayāna/Mahāyāna model is a fundamental distortion.

Once the term "Hīnayāna" turns out to be merely a dogmatic construct stemming from polemical discourse, the question arises: why has it been so widely used in the West by practitioners and scholars alike?

The widespread usage of the term "Hīnayāna" in Western publications appears to date back to the World's Parliament of Religions held in 1893 in Chicago, which had a decisive impact on the reception of Buddhism in the West. The Japanese delegation at this event promoted the term "Hīnayāna" as part of their attempt to establish the authenticity of Mahāyāna Buddhism (Anālayo 2016a: 483–89). From their viewpoint, Theravāda Buddhism was a form of Hīnayāna. Their presentation and the terminological usage established in this way had a lasting impact, in particular through the prolific writer D.T. Suzuki, a disciple of the Rinzai representative at the World's Parliament of Religions.

As in the case of the eighteen schools, in this case, too, the use of the term "Hīnayāna" emerges in a polemical setting. Another similarity is that, once again, it has no basis in reality. The aspiration to become a Buddha in the future is a well-known and accepted vocation in the Theravāda countries of Myanmar, Sri Lanka, and Thailand, attested to in inscriptions and texts as well as being actively practiced by some of its present-day eminent members (see, e.g., Rahula 1971, Ratnayaka 1985, Endo 1996, Samuels 1997, Skilling 2003, Harvey 2007, Chandawimala 2008, and for further references Anālayo 2016a: 491n51). Since some Theravādins practice the bodhisattva path, it is not proper to refer to the Theravāda traditions unilaterally as Hīnayāna. The main difference compared to Mahāyāna traditions is not that in the Theravāda traditions the bodhisattva path is not practiced at all, but only that it is not considered the solely viable form of practice.

As would have become evident from the material surveyed earlier in this chapter, the aspiration to become a Buddha oneself is the product of a gradual evolution, based on the separate emergence of various relevant ideas and notions in the course of oral transmission of the texts. For this reason, applying the term "Hīnayāna" to early Buddhism is an anachronism, since the generalized aspiration to become a Buddha in the future was not yet known in the early Buddhist period. The distinction between Hīnayāna and Mahāyāna presupposes the existence of the bodhisattva path as an ideal to be emulated, which one may either reject or else adopt. For such a decision to be possible and form the basis for a meaningful distinction, the bodhisattva ideal first of all has to come into existence.

In sum, to use the derogatory term "Hīnayāna" for a Buddhist school or institution is simply fiction.

12. The Superiority of the Mahāyāna

A problem with Hīnayāna rhetoric is that it can foster the conceit of superiority. Expressions of such conceit can be seen when the perceived difference in nature between bodhisattvas and those who do not pursue the path to Buddhahood is illustrated by comparing the latter to a jackal, who is unable to match a lion's roar, or to a donkey, who is incapable of carrying the load of an elephant (a *Mahāratnakūṭa* text; translated by Martini 2013: 37). The elephant motif to convey the same comparison recurs in a fifth-century meditation manual (by Kumārajīva; translated by Yamabe and Sueki 2009: 65). The manual contrasts a great elephant who crosses a rapid stream to monkeys and rabbits who are afraid of it, being concerned only with their own salvation.

A similar theme is the deep respect that should be accorded to anyone who has decided to pursue Buddhahood. According to one text, just as the son of a universal monarch will command the obeisance of all citizens as soon as he is born, so bodhisattvas deserve worldwide obeisance as soon as their aspiration for Buddhahood has been made (the *Kāśyapaparivarta*; translated by Pāsādika 2015: 148).

A closely related topic is the incomparability of aspiring to become Buddhas. Such bodhisattvas contrast to śrāvakas, a term used to denote those who have not embarked on the path to Buddhahood, whose "mind is limited, inferior, their faculties are very constrained, weak" (the *Book of Zambasta*; translated by Martini 2013: 29). In fact, śrāvakas cannot even dream of rivaling bodhisattvas, as the abilities of the latter are completely beyond the reach of the former (the *Vimalakīrtinirdeśa*; translated by Lamotte 1994: 228).

This incomparability holds even in relation to the central teaching of the four noble truths. Those who are not in pursuit of Buddhahood do not truly realize these, hence even the term "noble" is not really applicable to them (the *Śrīmālādevīsiṃhanāda-sūtra*; translated by Chang 1983: 377).

Another text recommends the thought "I shall achieve that which no other sentient being has achieved" (the *Bodhisattvapiṭaka*; translated by Pagel 1995: 403). The attitude underlying some such notions of the superiority of bodhisattvas can be conveniently summarized with the help of comments made by Nattier (2003: 146–47) on a particular formulation of the conception of the path to Buddhahood (in the *Ugraparipṛcchā*). This conception revolves around the

> stimulus to pursuing the bodhisattva path: the ambition of the practitioner himself ... of becoming the highest being in the universe ... a glorious prospect indeed. The bodhisattva is explicitly told that he should cultivate the thought that 'I must attain the body of a Buddha, ornamented with the thirty-two marks' ... and when he enters a monastery and pays homage to the Tathāgata he should reflect that 'I, too, should become one who is worthy of this kind of worship' ... [in sum,] part of the appeal of the bodhisattva path was the glory of striving for the highest achievement that the Buddhist repertoire had to offer. It is thus to the mentality of such people as Olympic athletes ('going for the gold') or Marine Corps recruits ('the few, the proud, the brave') that we probably should look if we want to understand what propelled these pioneering bodhisattvas to take on such a gargantuan task.

The comparison with Marine Corps recruits, presented by Jan Nattier, resonates with an illustration given in another text (the *Mahāparinirvāṇa-sūtra*; translated by Blum 2013: 240), according to which the attitude of a bodhisattva is akin to a person facing imminent battle whose state of mind is dominated by the thought, 'I am the person in front here. All the soldiers are depending entirely upon me.' This is also like a prince who ruminates, 'I will tame the other princes, continuing the work of great kings and hegemons . . . showing the other princes where their refuge lies.' Thus [a bodhisattva] should never give rise to thoughts of inferiority, just as kings, princes, or ministers cannot afford to do so.

In sum, as pointed out by Harrison (1995: 19), in some texts the bodhisattva ideal can involve

a kind of power fantasy, in which the Buddhist practitioner aspires not simply to the bare liberation or release of arhatship, but to the cosmic sovereignty and power represented by complete Buddhahood—not the destruction of ego, but its apotheosis.

13. Superior among Superiors

Claims to superiority and the corresponding condescending attitudes toward those considered inferior are not confined to the contrast between Mahāyāna and Hīnayāna. They can also occur in the context of rivalry between different Mahāyāna traditions. This can be seen in some strands of Vajrayāna, or Tantric Buddhism. The view of the hierarchical superiority of Vajrayāna can find an expression in the following manner (Tripiṭakamāla, summarized by Lopez 1996: 90):

followers of the Hīnayāna are confused about the nature of reality. Followers of the exoteric Mahāyāna understand emptiness but are confused about method, whereas the followers of the Mantrayāna are not confused about anything.

Expressed differently, "the *yānas* of Śrāvaka, *Pratyekabuddha*, and *Bodhisattva* are expounded to those of lesser (intellect)," whereas the

Vajrayāna "is called the summit of all the (*yānas*) . . . and the essence of the *yānas*" (Longchen Rabjam; translated by Thondup 1989/1996: 98–99). For this reason, someone "who accepts the Buddha as teacher but despises the Vajrayāna, which is the essence of his teaching," can be defined as a "Buddhist heretic" (Ratnākaraśānti's *Hevajrapañjikā muktāvalī*; summarized in Davidson 2002: 396n13).

The perceived need to relate later teachings in some way to the Buddha's awakening finds its expression in a narrative attributed to the time when the historical Buddha had approached the seat of awakening. He is roused from his sitting in absorption and informed that such practices do not suffice for him to become a perfect Buddha. His mind-made body is then conducted to the highest heaven where he receives the tantric consecrations indispensable for his attainment of Buddhahood (Snellgrove 1987/2002: 121). After having in this way become a perfect Buddha and having delivered tantric teachings on the mythical Mount Meru, he returns to earth to take possession again of his physical body and defeat Māra, a well-known motif depicted in traditional hagiography as preceding his actual awakening (see below p. 120).

A related strand emerges with the notion that a tantric teacher takes the place of the Buddha, evident in the injunction that one should understand that "the root lama is the essence of all buddhas, and that because the compassion of his very presence is accessible to you, he is even superior to them" (van Schaik 2014: 178). The sense of superiority can also be extended to practitioners of tantra in general, who are encouraged to identify themselves with all Buddhas (e.g. Tanemura 2009: 494–96). Such identification can even make it commendable to enjoin such practitioners not to worship Buddha statues, as to do so would violate their own status of being identical with all Buddhas (Wayman 1977: 259).

14. In Defense of the Mahāyāna

Out of the various forms of superiority claims among advocators of the bodhisattva path, the employment of Hīnayāna rhetoric as an expedient means to defend the authenticity of Mahāyāna teachings is of further relevance, as it reflects a tendency shared among different Buddhist traditions. This is the attempt to ascribe to the Buddha the authorship of texts considered sacred by one's own tradition, a topic to which I will return in the next chapter.

An illustrative instance of this attempt on behalf of Mahāyāna teachings can be found in a claim by Nanjio (1886: xiii), made in the context of providing a history of Japanese Buddhism. According to this claim, the first teaching delivered by the Buddha after his awakening was the *Buddhāvataṃsaka*, a text reflecting a mature stage of Mahāyāna thought and cosmology. Since Nanjio had studied under Max Müller at Oxford, his claim came endowed with the credentials of academic scholarship. It reflects a traditional expedient of relegating so-called Hīnayāna teachings to a later period in the Buddha's teaching career, subsequent to his presumed original delivery of Mahāyāna teachings.

In light of the progress of academic research on the history and evolution of Buddhist texts, it is no longer feasible to maintain such attributions to the historical Buddha (made similarly by Theravādins for some of their later texts). An illustrative example is a text particularly popular among Mahāyāna Buddhist traditions, usually referred to as the Heart Sūtra. According to academic research, this text appears to have been originally composed in Chinese and only subsequently rendered into Sanskrit (Nattier 1992 and Attwood 2018).

The speaker of this text, the bodhisattva Avalokiteśvara, is unknown to the early Buddhist texts. His being depicted as addressing Śāriputra, who in the early discourses features as the foremost disciple of the Buddha, does not make the contents of this scripture any earlier; Sāriputta has been appropriated by later traditions in various ways. His eminence in wisdom and analysis made him a convenient icon for the early Abhidharma traditions. Hence, it is only natural that texts critical of Abhidharma tendencies toward reification similarly appropriate his name, casting him in the role of a disciple receiving teachings to counter such tendencies. Both usages concern a literary figure.

The sheer impossibility of attributing this scripture to the period in which the Buddha would have lived raises the question of how far the Heart Sūtra's appeal to profundity depends on the nationality of its composer(s) and the time it came into being. The perceived need to authenticate scripture by recourse to ahistorical presumptions is a tendency shared among different Buddhist traditions and not a problem of followers of the Mahāyāna alone. This makes it all the more pertinent to free the appreciation and religious use of a particular text from such tactics. In the present case, the task would be to find ways to apply the medicine of emptiness to the Heart Sūtra itself, in order to provide a cure for the perceived need of resorting to questionable authentication strategies.

SUMMARY

Descriptions of the Buddha's special bodily marks appear to be the result of a cross-fertilization between texts and art, where textual descriptions were concretized in pictorial depiction, which in turn inspired textual literalism. From being initially conceived as subtle nuances beyond the ken of the untrained observer, over the course of time the marks came to be imagined as more easily visible. Relating these marks to conditionality by way of associating each mark to a particular type of conduct observed in past lives appears to have set the stage for the emergence of the notion that the path to Buddhahood requires cultivation during previous lifetimes.

The motif of the future Buddha Maitreya can be identified as a later development, resulting from an embellishment of a parable that originally would have had no particular relationship to past or future Buddhas. An additional occurrence of the same motif in an evidently late part of another discourse depicts a monastic aspiring to become the future Buddha Maitreya. Such aspiration has a counterpart in another late element found in a different discourse, which reports that the Buddha Gotama took his original vow to become a Buddha himself in the future when he was a monastic under the previous Buddha Kassapa.

In the early texts, a predominant concern with his own liberation rather than with the liberation of others is evident in the accounts of the Buddha Gotama's initial motivation to set out in search of awakening and his successful completion of this quest. The idea that the aspiration to become a Buddha has as its core element the wish to save sentient beings is a later development. The early Buddhist conception of compassion, as one of a set of four sublime mental attitudes, focuses on the prospect of allaying harm, rather than on emphatically taking unto oneself the pain of others.

The rhetoric of self-sacrifice for the sake of others that can accompany notions of compassion in later texts has at times led to rather drastic enactments. The practice of setting parts or the whole of one's own body on fire may have its origin in a literalist reading of a verse that originally employed only the image of a burning spark becoming extinct to illustrate the freedom from future rebirth gained by arahants.

Another late element in an early discourse involves a declaration of worldwide superiority made by the infant Buddha immediately after his birth. Probably the result of applying a description of the Buddha's post-awakening condition to the period of his infancy, the resultant passage sets a precedent for a sense of the inherent superiority of bodhisattvas.

Such a sense of superiority may have provided a congenial environment for the arising of the idea that the mind is already intrinsically awakened. This notion appears to be related to a passage that applies the idea of the mind's luminosity to a contrast between a defiled and an undefiled condition of the mind, with the net result that the mind's luminosity remains even when defilements are present.

The need for an authentication of Mahāyāna texts as teachings of the historical Buddha appears to be responsible for the emergence of Hīnayāna rhetoric. The distinction between those who follow the bodhisattva path and those who do not aspire to future Buddhahood is a vocational one and needs to be differentiated from monastic ordination taken in any of what are conventionally called the eighteen schools of Buddhism. The usage of the term "Hīnayāna" has its origin in polemics and lacks a grounding in the historical reality of Indian Buddhism. It cannot be used to refer to the Theravāda traditions, as some Theravādins have been and still are practitioners of the bodhisattva path. Nor can it be applied to early Buddhism, as during that period the bodhisattva path had not yet come into existence. This leaves no basis for the application of a term that concerns the decision whether or not to pursue such a path.

The employment of the term "Hīnayāna" has a counterpart in claims to the superiority of bodhisattvas, actively encouraged in various texts through comparisons and illustrations expressive of contempt for those who are not in pursuit of Buddhahood. The same tendency to belittling can also find employment in the context of rivalry among different Mahāyāna traditions. Besides the need to set aside the term "Hīnayāna" in clear recognition of its polemical origins, historical unreality, and discriminatory nature, there is also a need to leave behind the underlying attempt to authenticate scripture through untenable attributions to the historical Buddha.

In sum, the significant contributions made by Mahāyāna thought to Buddhism would shine forth more brightly if they could be divested of the blemish of superiority conceit.

III. Theravāda Buddhism

INTRODUCTION

IN THIS CHAPTER I study a form of superiority conceit found among some Theravāda Buddhists. This takes the form of assuming that membership in the Theravāda tradition automatically implies being the true heir to the Buddha's original teachings. In order to show that this notion lacks a foundation, I examine in some detail the Path of Purification, the *Visuddhimagga*, a key manual of the path compiled by Buddhaghosa in the fifth century. Even though the nature of my exploration in this chapter necessitates that I focus on several aspects of this work that involve some departure from early Buddhist thought, pointing these out is not meant to imply a wholesale rejection. Buddhaghosa's masterpiece remains a central reference for anyone cultivating Theravāda meditation practice. My point is only that this work offers a distinctly Theravāda perspective, which at times differs from the early Buddhist position.

I begin with the contrast drawn in a Ceylonese chronicle between the Theravāda and other traditions in light of what appear to have been the historical conditions that led to a tendency toward conservatism in the early stages of Sri Lankan Buddhism. Then I survey various instances when the Theravāda tradition has come to take positions that differ from early Buddhism. A topic that already came up in the last chapter is the acceptance of the bodhisattva ideal (see p. 64). Another relevant position is the widespread belief among later generations of Buddhists that the Buddha was omniscient. The notion of the comprehensiveness of knowledge that underlies the idea of omniscience appears to have been a central undercurrent in the arising of Abhidharma, which the Theravādins—just as other Buddhist traditions—consider to have been taught by the historical Buddha himself. This attribution involves forms of textual authentication similar to those evident in Mahāyāna Buddhist traditions, discussed in the previous chapter (see p. 68).

Shifts in perspective from early Buddhism to Theravāda affect the understanding of mindfulness as well as its cultivation when observing the breath. Changing understandings are similarly evident in the meditative development of the divine abodes. Differences in viewpoints can also be discerned in relation to key doctrines of early Buddhist thought, namely dependent arising, impermanence, *dukkha*, and not self. In addition, I take up an apparent error made by Buddhaghosa when adopting a scheme of seven stages of purification as the basic scaffolding for his *Visuddhimagga*.

Distinct Theravāda viewpoints on meditation-related topics, found in the *Visuddhimagga*, have in turn influenced contemporary meditation teachings. They stand in the background of current *vipassanā* meditation traditions that have provided the starting point for the global spread of secular applications of mindfulness. An apparently polemical move by the proponents of *vipassanā* meditation to defend themselves against accusations of side-stepping the cultivation of absorption, which was perceived by others as an indispensable requirement for progress to awakening, seems to have set the scene for a reinterpretation of the nature of absorption in current times. In this way, differing perspectives keep emerging from ancient to modern times, showing that Theravāda doctrines and practices have evolved and continue to evolve in response to various causes and conditions. Although in itself only natural, this undermines the superiority conceit of assuming that the Theravāda tradition is the sole true representative of what the Buddha originally taught.

1. THERAVĀDA

The term *theravāda* already occurs in a Pāli discourse. Here it refers to teachings the future Buddha Gotama acquired during his apprenticeship with his two teachers Āḷāra Kālāma and Uddaka Rāmaputta, proponents of the higher two of altogether four immaterial attainments (translated by

Ñāṇamoli 1995/2005: 257). Notably, this earliest attested occurrence of the term *theravāda* refers to non-Buddhist teachings (Anālayo 2016a: 499).

A Sri Lankan chronicle, called the *Dīpavaṃsa*, employs the term *theravāda* for the teachings that according to the traditional account were collected at the first "communal recitation," *saṅgīti*, mentioned already in previous chapters (translated by Oldenberg 1879: 134). The same work claims that seventeen of the so-called eighteen Buddhist schools are schismatic, the Theravāda being the one orthodox school (translated by Oldenberg 1879: 142).

A "schism" requires an intentional act by a group of at least four monastics who no longer undertake communal observances together with the other members of what until then was their monastic community. The emergence of different monastic traditions in India, however, appears to be rather the outcome of geographical separation and the gradual accumulation of differences in the orally transmitted monastic codes. The resultant monastic traditions are neither the result of schism nor are they chiefly "sects" in a dogmatic sense (Anālayo 2020d). Instead, such schools or *nikāya*s, whatever their actual number, are essentially different lineages of monastic observance, none of which can rightfully claim to be invariably more orthodox than the others.

The proverbial conservatism of Theravādins may in turn be the result of historical conditions. In the Indian setting, continuous competition with other religious groups was responsible for a need to keep adapting in order to be able to respond to any challenge. This was even more the case when Buddhist traditions spread to Central Asia and China, where they needed to adjust to substantially different cultures. In the case of Sri Lanka, however, there was considerably less need for such adaptation. Sri Lankan culture did not differ from Indian civilization in a way comparable to that of Central Asia or China, nor was there a strongly developed and sufficiently sophisticated indigenous culture that demanded constant adjustment. Hence, there was less need for adaptation and innovation, naturally fostering the emergence of a conservative sense of identity.

The resultant tendency toward conservatism among Sri Lankan Theravādins became further strengthened during a period of rivalry between two influential monasteries, called the Mahāvihāra and the Abhayagirivi-hāra. In the context of a struggle for primacy between these two monaster-ies in Sri Lanka, the more conservatively oriented Mahāvihāra entrusted Buddhaghosa with the task of translating the Sinhala commentaries on the Pāli canonical scriptures into Pāli. The appeal of his *Visuddhimagga*, probably the most influential compendium of Theravāda doctrine and practice, and of his translations of the commentaries into Pāli further fortified the tendency toward conservatism.

In this way, the conservatism of the Theravāda traditions appears, at least to some extent, to be the accidental result of historical circum-stances. It does not imply that the Theravāda school is the sole nonschis-matic school and the only custodian of Buddhism in its original form.

At the same time, it does not follow that the usage of the term "Thera-vāda" as such needs to be problematized in order to counter such notions (Anālayo 2016a: 508–22). After all, we do not problematize terms like "United States of America," even though the country so called does not unite the whole territory of the Americas, nor do we dispute the right of the Chinese to consider themselves the "central country" (*Zhongguo*), even though there is no reason for considering China to be the center of the world. Similarly, the established use of the name "Theravāda" by the members of this tradition should be respected. The point is only to acknowledge that Theravāda doctrinal positions can at times differ from early Buddhism, as will become evident in the remainder of this chapter. Hence, these two historical layers of Buddhism need to be differentiated from each other, rather than being equated with each other.

2. PĀLI

In line with the step taken by the Mahāvihāra of having the commentar-ies translated into Pāli, a key characteristic uniting different Theravāda traditions is the employment of Pāli as their sacred language. The *Visud-dhimagga* considers Pāli to be endowed with its own essence (*sabhāva*) and to be the root language of all beings (Ñāṇamoli 1991: 441). Such a position does not align well with the attitude toward language evident in the early discourses. Deokar (2012: 119–21) reasons

The Buddha redefined the concept of pure or good speech by giving prominence to the intention and contents of the language over its outer form . . . the Buddha also rejected adherence to any particular language or expression. He opposed the idea of a single sacred language and asked his followers to give up insistence on the provincial dialect . . .

However, it was very difficult for the Buddha's disciples to maintain the same attitude towards the language of his teaching, i.e. Māgadhī or Pāli, once it assumed the form of a standard sacred language . . . the Theravāda tradition, in line with the Vedic tradition, also attached significance to correct . . . speech especially during religious performances and monastic legal matters.

The concern with correct wording is a fairly pervasive characteristic of Theravāda monasticism. It goes so far as to require that a candidate for ordination recite the traditional refuge formula twice, with different pronunciations, to ensure that, one way or the other, the recital will be correct (Anālayo 2017i: 248–49). When referring to the Buddha as the object of the first refuge, for example, the difference to be enacted in this way concerns saying either *buddham* or *buddhang*, as two alternative ways of articulating the nasal sound in the term *buddhaṃ*. From a traditional Theravāda perspective, by employing both ways of pronunciation the correct performance of the ritual act of taking refuge has been ensured and thereby the necessary basis has been established for the correct undertaking of the ordination procedure.

During the actual ordination, the candidate and the preceptor assume the fictive names Nāga and Tissa to avoid possible mispronunciations if their real proper names were to be declined in accordance with Pāli grammar (Anālayo 2017i: 246). In this way, for centuries ordinations in Theravāda traditions have been granted with exactly the same formula by an unending series of Tissas ordaining a similarly unending series of Nāgas, even though the actual persons involved of course had different names and resumed these once the ordination was over. As noted by von Hinüber (1987/1994: 228):

Here it is perhaps not too far-fetched to assume the influence of the recitation of Vedic texts . . . for, in the same way as the magical effect of the Vedic *mantras* is guaranteed only if not even the slightest mistake has been made in pronouncing them, likewise the validity of the *kammavācās* [statements of legal acts] is established in Buddhist law by exactly the same accuracy in pronunciation.

3. The Bodhisattva Ideal

Regarding the nature of the Pāli discourses, Salomon (2018: 56) comments that

> early scholars of Buddhism in the West, especially in the English-speaking world, had assumed that the Pali canon represented *the* true original scriptures of Buddhism while other manifestations of Buddhism and versions of Buddhist texts were secondary derivations, elaborations, or corruptions. This view prevailed mainly because the Pali canon of the Theravāda tradition of Sri Lanka and Southeast Asia happened to be the only one that survived complete and intact in an Indian language, and because it came to the attention of Anglophone scholars at a relatively early date as a result of the colonization of Sri Lanka by England. This led to the illusion that the Pali canon was the only true Buddhist canon, and the misconception was reinforced by the self-presentation of the bearers of that tradition, who were the early European scholars' main points of contact with the Buddhist world. But it is now clear that the seeming primacy and authority of the Pali Tipiṭaka is only an accident of history.

Examples illustrating this assessment have already emerged in the course of the previous chapter, in the form of Pāli discourses testifying to the gradual evolution of the bodhisattva ideal. Such occurrences imply that later developments can at times manifest in Pāli canonical texts, just as they can manifest in the discourses of other traditions.

As already mentioned in the previous chapter, the acceptance of the bodhisattva ideal is also not confined to Mahāyāna traditions, but has similarly become an integral part of the living Theravāda traditions in Myanmar, Sri Lanka, and Thailand alike, attested in inscriptions and texts (see p. 64). A noteworthy difference is that the bodhisattva ideal is not considered invariably superior to the aim to reach arahantship, as both types of goals are considered viable and worthwhile options.

Another aspiration of remarkable appeal among Theravāda monastics appears to have been the wish to be reborn at the time of the Buddha Maitreya and personally witness his future glories. The advent of this future Buddha involves another notion attested in a Pāli discourse that, judging from a comparative study of the parallel versions, is a later element (see p. 48).

The *Visuddhimagga* relates the story of a senior monastic on his deathbed who until then had not reached any level of awakening (Ñāṇamoli 1991: 47). Questioned by other monastics, he explained that he had the aspiration to be reborn at the time of the Buddha Maitreya. Admonished by the other monastics to make an effort to progress to liberation, he sat up with their help and reached full awakening right there and then. The story implies that his spiritual faculties and abilities had been highly developed, yet, due to his wish to meet Maitreya, he had not put them to service to reach awakening until he was on the brink of death. In addition to relating the story of this monastic, Buddhaghosa also concludes his *Visuddhimagga* by expressing his own aspiration to be reborn, after a life spent in heaven, at the time of the future Buddha Maitreya (Ñāṇamoli 1991: 743).

In line with the traditional belief that the Buddha himself had pursued the path of a bodhisattva, the *Visuddhimagga* refers to his aspiration for future Buddhahood made in the presence of the former Buddha Dīpaṅkara (Ñāṇamoli 1991: 199). Figure 7 shows a pictorial depiction of successive moments in the meeting between the former Buddha Dīpaṅkara and the one who was to become the Buddha Gotama: the bodhisattva buys

Figure 7. Successive scenes in the meeting between the future
Buddha Gotama and the Buddha Dīpaṅkara; Gandhāra.

flowers, scatters them over Dīpaṅkara, and finally spreads his hair on the
ground for the Buddha Dīpaṅkara to step on.

4. The Buddha's Omniscience

Besides accepting the distinctly late notion that the Buddha himself
followed the path of a bodhisattva during a series of previous lives, the
Visuddhimagga also considers him to have been omniscient (translated by
Ñāṇamoli 1991: 198). This belief, held in common by a range of Buddhist
traditions, lacks support in the early discourses (Anālayo 2014b: 117–24
and 2020e). A Pāli discourse, of which no parallel is known, reports the
Buddha being directly questioned as to whether he had claimed to be
omniscient (translated by Ñāṇamoli 1995/2005: 587). In reply, the Buddha clarifies that this is a misrepresentation, as he claimed only to have

attained the three higher knowledges. These are recollection of his own past lives, witnessing the passing away and being reborn of others, and the eradication of the unwholesome influxes in his mind.

Another passage relevant to the notion of omniscience involves the Buddha's personal attendant Ānanda, who points out various problems with claims to being all-knowing (translated by Ñāṇamoli 1995/2005: 623). Since omniscience in the ancient Indian setting implied knowledge of the future, a claimant to such knowledge is forced to resort to evasive arguments when meeting with some kind of adversity or misfortune. Examples are approaching an empty house for alms, being bitten by a dog or encountering other wild animals, or having to ask the name of a person or a village. Being endowed with omniscient knowledge, any such episode could have been avoided and ignorance should not have manifested in the first place. Hence, the claimant to omniscience has to assert that it was necessary to approach that empty house, knowing all the while that no alms could be received there, etc. The discourse concludes that following a teacher who makes such claims is to embark on a spiritual life that offers no consolation.

The reasoning presented here could similarly be applied to some adversities or misfortunes encountered by the Buddha himself (some of which Ānanda, due to being his personal attendant, must have been aware of). A related problem emerges when turning to the *Vinaya*, the texts on monastic discipline. As pointed out by Gombrich (2007: 206f),

> the idea that the Buddha was omniscient is strikingly at odds with the picture of him presented in every *Vinaya* tradition ... not only does the entire *Vinaya* tradition show that the Buddha did not anticipate what rules would be needed, he even occasionally made a false start and found it necessary to reverse a decision. Since omniscience includes knowledge of the future, this is not omniscience. A pious Buddhist who was committed to believing that the Buddha was omniscient would have to say that his ignorance of the future was a charade. This would raise a problem about his truthfulness.

5. Authenticating the Abhidharma

The Buddha's assumed omniscience appears to have been one of the chief strands that influenced the emergence of Abhidharma thought. This significant development does not appear to be merely the product of formal elements, such as summaries (*māṭikā*) or question and answer exchanges (Anālayo 2014b: 21–28). Instead, a central driving force seems to have been the attempt to provide a comprehensive map of the teachings, similar in thrust to the notion of omniscience that had eventually been attributed to the Buddha.

Comparable to the beginnings of the bodhisattva ideal, initial stages of Abhidharma thought can be discerned through comparative study of the early discourses (Anālayo 2014b). Besides being invested with an increasing aura of supremacy, the gradually emerging corpus of Abhidharma teachings also needed to be authenticated as stemming from the historical Buddha himself. For this purpose, members of the Theravāda traditions employed the same strategies, be this intentionally or in the sincere belief that such teachings indeed stemmed from the Buddha, that they have tended to criticize in the case of their Mahāyāna brethren.

The way Theravādins solve the problem of authenticating the Abhidharma can be seen in the *Visuddhimagga*'s account of a sojourn of the Buddha in the Heaven of the Thirty-Three, during which he purportedly taught the Abhidharma to the denizens of heaven (translated by Ñāṇamoli 1991: 387). Buddhaghosa relates that the Buddha would daily repeat, in the presence of his human disciple Sāriputta, what he had just taught to the denizens of heaven. In this way, the transmission of the Abhidharma was ensured.

The *Visuddhimagga* also reports that the ruler of the Heaven of the Thirty-Three built a flight of stairs for the Buddha's descent back to earth, after the completion of his sojourn of three months in heaven (translated by Ñāṇamoli 1991: 388). Given his earlier easy commutation to heaven by supernormal powers, it is unexpected that his descent would require stairs. Closer inspection of relevant material gives the impression that this idea would have resulted from a process of cross-fertilization between text and art (Anālayo 2015d: 424–29), similar to the development of some of

Figure 8. The Buddha descends from heaven, flanked by celestials; Myinkaba Kubyauggyi, Pagan.

the Buddha's physical marks, discussed in the previous chapter (see p. 45). During an early period of "aniconic" depiction of the Buddha, a ladder or a flight of stairs would have been an obvious way to symbolize that he is descending. Such symbolic presentation appears to have been taken literally by later generations, leading to the idea that there must have been an actual flight of stairs by which the Buddha descended from heaven. Figure 8 shows the employment of a kind of ladder on which the Buddha descends to earth, after the completion of his three-month period of teaching Abhidharma in heaven.

6. THE FIVE AGGREGATES AND MINDFULNESS

A key feature in the evolution of Abhidharma thought is the attempt to be as comprehensive as possible. The shift of perspective that emerges in this way can be illustrated with an analysis of subjective experience into five "aggregates of clinging." These are body, feeling tone, perception, volitional formations, and consciousness. In the early discourses, this analytical scheme serves to highlight what unawakened beings tend to cling to as manifestations of a sense of self. In the context of the five-aggregate analysis, the fourth aggregate of formations stands in particular for volition and will power.

With the shift to a more Abhidharma-oriented perspective, the same five aggregates of clinging became a scaffolding for assembling various terms describing aspects of subjective experience. Informed by this shift of perspective, the aggregate of "volitional formations" came to serve as an umbrella term for a whole range of various mental factors, independent of whether these carry a self-evident relationship to the exercise of volition (Anālayo 2010a: 43). This tendency can be seen in the list the *Visuddhimagga* provides for the fourth aggregate (translated by Ñāṇamoli 1991: 465). Besides volition, this list contains a range of mental factors and qualities, including, for example, mindfulness.

Just as with other members of this list, mindfulness is not a natural fit for the category of volitional formations. This holds in particular for the early Buddhist notion of mindfulness. In fact, the understanding of this particular mental quality also appears to have undergone some change over the course of time. This can be seen in the *Visuddhimagga*'s explanation of the import of this term, given subsequent to the above listing. This explanation proposes that mindfulness has the characteristic of "not floating" (*apilāpana*).

The term employed in this context already occurs in a Pāli discourse in a context related to mindfulness (translated by Bodhi 2012: 561), where the corresponding verb appears to stand for the ability to remember something that one had earlier memorized. With Abhidharma and exegetical Pāli texts, however, the term underwent a change of meaning. Instead of being seen as a compound of *api* + *lāpana*, the term was interpreted to be a combination of *a* + *pilāpana* (Norman 1988: 49–51 and Gethin 1992: 37–40). Consequently, it came to convey the sense of "not floating" and hence led to the idea that mindfulness plunges into whatever objects are taken up by the mind. This invests mindfulness with an active and forward-thrusting connotation that is not found in early Buddhist texts (Anālayo 2019c), where it appears to be more a receptive and noninterfering form of awareness.

7. Mindfulness of Breathing

The practice of mindfulness of breathing also seems to have changed to some degree, a change affecting different practice traditions and therefore not being confined to Theravādins. The starting point for such an apparent process of change can be found in instructions given in the early discourses on mindfulness of breathing in sixteen steps (Anālayo 2019h). These sixteen steps fall into four tetrads of four steps each. Whereas the first tetrad comes with an emphasis on bodily dimensions of the experience of the breath, meditative steps in the second and third tetrads encourage the cultivation of joy, happiness, and gladness, whose skillful employment leads to a natural calming of the mind. In this way, the canonical instructions on mindfulness of breathing make intelligent use of a basic principle repeatedly mentioned elsewhere in the early discourses, according to which the arousing of nonsensual types of joy and happiness can lead the mind naturally into tranquility and concentration.

In the course of the oral transmission of the early discourses, the first tetrad of these instructions appears to have been taken out of its original setting and added as an additional exercise to expositions on various ways of contemplating the body with mindfulness. In itself this is a natural development, since the first tetrad indeed corresponds to a mindful contemplation of a bodily phenomenon. As a result, however, the relationship to the ensuing steps concerned with joy, happiness, and gladness as what leads on to calmness and concentration is no longer fully evident. Further reduction led to an emphasis on only the first two steps and eventually to a focus on just the breath as such, to the exclusion of anything else (Anālayo 2019f).

As a net result of such developments, it is unsurprising if supplementary tools were developed in order to aid the practitioner in actualizing the frequently mentioned potential of mindfulness of breathing to bring about the absence of mental distraction. The diminished emphasis on the skillful employment of nonsensual joy and happiness was apparently compensated for by introducing additional techniques, in particular counting the breaths as a way to develop concentration. Such counting of the breaths is only found in later texts. Although it can indeed be helpful for some practitioners, the potential of progressing through the whole scheme of sixteen steps of mindfulness of breathing to lead naturally to concentration has to some extent receded into the background. This progression came to be seen as requiring that one has already mastered concentration, for which purpose one then relies on counting the breaths.

8. THE DIVINE ABODES

Another shift in the mode of meditation practice from early Buddhism to Theravāda can be discerned in relation to the divine abodes (*brahmavihāra*), comprising benevolence or loving kindness (*mettā*), compassion, sympathetic joy, and equanimity. The early discourses regularly describe the meditative cultivation of these divine abodes as a radiation in all directions. The unlimited nature of this radiation, free from any obstructions, finds reflection in an alternative term that designates these four sublime mental attitudes as "boundless" (*appamāṇa*).

Later tradition considers such radiation to describe absorption attainment. This does not seem to hold for the early discourses, a perusal of which suggests that a radiation of the divine abodes can take place at levels well below absorption attainment (Anālayo 2015a: 20–26). An instructive episode concerns a brahmin who is taught, apparently for the first time in his life, the meditative cultivation of the divine abodes while on his deathbed (translated by Ñāṇamoli 1995/2005: 796). Previously, this brahmin had been engaging in immoral conduct. The way the discourse describes him does not give the impression that he was a meditator, let alone someone with the meditative expertise that would be required for the attainment of absorption (Anālayo 2017c: 109–75). After being in grave pain until the time of his death, according to the discourse's report he was reborn in the Brahmā world. Such a rebirth fits the case of someone who has successfully cultivated the divine abodes, which implies that the brahmin had indeed been able to put to good use the instructions on their radiation he had just received.

In later Theravāda tradition, however, the approach to the cultivation of the divine abodes focuses on individual persons as objects and the radiation requires first developing this person-oriented approach. For the case of benevolence or loving kindness, for example, meditative cultivation should start by taking first oneself as the object, then someone dear, then someone neutral, and finally a hostile person (Ñāṇamoli 1991: 290).

A person-oriented approach for the cultivation of the divine abodes is also found in other Buddhist traditions, although recommended for those who are unable to practice the radiation due to the presence of some defilement in the mind. The idea of directing benevolence (*mettā*) first of all to oneself seems to be specific to the Theravāda tradition, however, perhaps the result of a literal reading of a textual variant (Anālayo 2015b: 15–21). This textual variant involves a Pāli term that occurs in the standard description of the meditative radiation. The two extant variants of the term mean either "in every way" or else "to all as to oneself." The context and extant parallel versions make it safe to conclude that the original sense was "in every way," serving to qualify the all-pervasive nature of the radiation. The idea of directing *mettā* to oneself, however, relies on the alternative meaning as "to all as to oneself."

In this way, the meditative cultivation of the divine abodes appears to have undergone some change in perspective, just as mindfulness of breathing. Pointing out such developments is not meant in any way to put into question meditation practice done in this way. Reliance on individual persons as objects for *mettā* and on counting to keep the mind with the breath must be highly beneficial, otherwise they would hardly have been employed so widely. Here and elsewhere, the point is only to show that there have been shifts in perspective from the early Buddhist approach to current Theravāda practice, without intending to encourage thereby a wholesale dismissal of the latter.

Some shifts in perspective are also to some degree evident in relation to the meditative cultivation of insight. These can best be illustrated by taking up prominent themes for insightful inspection: dependent arising and the three characteristics of impermanence, *dukkha*, and not self.

9. DEPENDENT ARISING

The doctrine of dependent arising stands at the core of the early Buddhist teachings, to the extent that one who sees dependent arising sees the Dharma (translated by Ñāṇamoli 1995/2005: 283). This statement appears to intend a penetrative seeing with insight of the principle of dependent arising (*paṭicca samuppāda*), as distinct from dependently arisen things (Anālayo 2020c). Another discourse distinguishes between this principle and things that are dependently arisen, the latter being regularly mentioned links of dependent arising, like ignorance, formations, consciousness, name-and-form, etc., (translated by Bodhi 2000: 551). The standard exposition of such dependently arisen things appears to stand in dialogue with a Vedic creation myth (Jurewicz 2000). In other words, this particular application of dependent arising seems to respond to ideas current in the ancient Indian setting.

The basic principle of dependent arising, on the other hand, refers to the specific conditionality that operates in relation to each of the links, as a result of which a preceding link is an indispensable condition for the arising of the next one. It follows that the removal of that preceding link will result in the cessation of the next one. This is precisely the main concern of the teaching on dependent arising: to bring about the cessation of the conditions productive of *dukkha*.

Later Theravāda tradition expounds dependent arising by way of twenty-four types of conditions, in the belief that these twenty-four were taught by the Buddha (translated by Ñāṇamoli 1991: 542). This set of twenty-four conditions is not found in the early discourses and emerges only in a comparatively late book of the canonical Abhidharma of the Theravāda tradition, the *Paṭṭhāna*.

The set of twenty-four conditions resulting from this procedure has acquired high regard in Theravāda circles and regularly forms the basis of ceremonial recitation. From the viewpoint of "seeing" dependent arising with insight, however, an analysis of the twelve links by way of twenty-four conditions can have an effect similar to the expansion of the fourth aggregate of clinging, discussed above. In both cases, there is a danger that the chief implication of the respective teaching becomes buried under excessive detail. In the words of Ñāṇananda (2015: 560),

> [the] confusion regarding the way of explaining *paṭicca samup-pāda* [dependent arising] is a case of missing the wood for the trees. It is as if the Buddha stretches his arm and says: "That is a forest," and one goes and catches hold of a tree, exclaiming: "Ah, this is the forest."

10. Momentariness

What is dependently arisen must necessarily be impermanent. As a correlate of conditionality, impermanence is the first of three characteristics that are of central importance for the cultivation of liberating insight. Here, too, a shift in understanding from early Buddhism to later traditions can be discerned, taking the form of the notion of momentariness.

The basic idea of momentariness is that whatever arises will disappear immediately. This differs from the conception of impermanence in early Buddhism, which recognizes that something arisen may persist for some time as a changing process before it disappears (Anālayo 2013b: 105–108 and 2018d: 12). A teaching on the three marks of what is conditioned, for example, points out an arising, a passing away, and an alteration while persisting (translated by Bodhi 2012: 246). The same principle finds repeated application in relation to feeling tones, perceptions, and thoughts, whose persistence as impermanent processes should be known just as much as their arising and passing away (translated by Walshe 1987:

488, Ñāṇamoli 1995/2005: 983, Bodhi 2000: 1657, and Bodhi 2012: 432, 1023, and 1122).

With the radicalization of impermanence in the form of the doctrine of momentariness, however, the continuity of things as changing phenomena came to be effaced. The evident fact of alteration was seen as a series of momentary replacements. In some strands of this doctrine, for example, the gradual coloring of a cloth was conceptualized as involving a quick succession of a series of pieces of cloth, each slightly more colored than the previous one (von Rospatt 1995: 169). Or else the burning of wood was thought to involve a series of logs of wood that replace each other, each one being just slightly more charred than the previous one (von Rospatt 1995: 183).

The widespread appeal of the doctrine of momentariness among Buddhist traditions led to further developments, such as the introduction of some aspect of the mind that can explain memory in the face of rapidly passing away mental moments. In the Theravāda tradition, this took the form of what could perhaps be rendered as the "life-continuum," the *bhavaṅga citta* (Gethin 1994).

The problem posed by momentariness can be illustrated with a recommendation in the *Visuddhimagga* for countering anger (translated by Ñāṇamoli 1991: 293). The advice, given in verse form, takes as its point of departure the momentary nature of the five aggregates. One should reflect that the other person's aggregates, having done something unpleasing, have already ceased. Hence, with whom or what could one be getting angry?

The reasoning proposed here disregards the fact of continuity. If the same were to be applied to wholesome acts and the principle of karma and its fruit, it would result in denying a causal relationship beyond the actual moment when something takes place. Of course, this is only a reflection meant to counter anger. In fact, the *Visuddhimagga* continues by proposing that, in case this method has not been successful, one should rely on reflecting that oneself and the other are both heirs of their karma. This alternative approach to removing anger avoids the potential problems of the previous approach, as it relies on ideas that can without difficulty be applied in a different context.

11. DUKKHA

Comparable to the case of impermanence, in relation to *dukkha* as the second of the two characteristics some shift in perspective can also be seen in later Buddhist traditions. An example would be a sequence of experiences recognized in Theravāda texts as "insight knowledges," which meditators are expected to go through in their progress to stream entry, the first of the four levels of awakening. The listing of such insight knowledges can be considered a more detailed working out of a basic pattern already evident in the early discourses, based on the three characteristics (Anālayo 2012a). According to this basic pattern, anything that is impermanent is for this reason incapable of providing lasting satisfaction; it is *dukkha*. What is impermanent and *dukkha* does not qualify for being reckoned a self. The last reasoning is based on the notion of a self in ancient India, where it stood for a permanent and inherently blissful entity.

As part of a more detailed elaboration of aspects of *dukkha* in the course of depicting the progress of liberating insight, Theravāda exegesis introduced the insight knowledge of fear. Setting in after a mature stage of insight into impermanence has been reached, the knowledge of fear finds illustration in several comparisons (Ñāṇamoli 1991: 668). One of these describes a timid person who either encounters a dangerous wild animal (such as a lion, a tiger, a bear, a fierce bull, a wild elephant in rut, or a venomous serpent) or else faces something terrifying (such as a ghost, a thunderbolt, a cemetery, or a battlefield). This is meant to illustrate the degree to which everything appears fearful to a meditator at this advanced stage in the cultivation of insight. The early discourses, in contrast, do not recognize an insight knowledge of fear as an indispensable part of progress in liberating insight (Anālayo 2019e: 2175–78).

The tendency to place excessive emphasis on negative aspects finds a convenient illustration in the pervasive translation of *dukkha* as "suffering" (Anālayo 2003: 244–45). The widespread reliance on this translation can lead to the erroneous conclusion that the key teaching of Buddhism is: "everything is suffering."

Suffering is a reaction of an untrained mind, not a quality inherent in things in the world. Impermanent phenomena are *dukkha* in the sense of being unsatisfactory. But whether that leads to suffering depends on how someone reacts to manifestations of impermanence. Even painful feeling tones are not necessarily suffering. With mindfulness established, it becomes possible to experience physical pain without mental suffering (Anālayo 2016c). Nor is the changing nature of feeling tones automatically a matter of suffering. When a pleasant feeling tone changes, this may call up reactions of suffering in an untrained mind, but not in an accomplished practitioner. When a painful feeling tone changes, this will hardly result in suffering, whether or not the one who experiences such change has ever meditated.

12. Not Self

In early Buddhist thought, the doctrine of not self refers to the absence of a permanent entity in subjective experience. It follows from the pervasive applicability of impermanence and conditionality. Once all aspects of subjective experience are impermanent and conditioned, there cannot be an unchanging self anywhere. The same doctrine is also closely related to the teaching on dependent arising, which implies that the entire range of ordinary experience is nothing but a combination of causes and conditions. This dispenses with any substantial or permanent entity anywhere.

However, in its original formulation, the doctrine of not self does not mean that nothing exists at all. It means only that, whatever is there, is impermanent and conditioned, being for this reason not fit to be considered a self.

The emergence of a somewhat different perspective can be discerned in the *Visuddhimagga*'s proposal that, given that a chariot is made up of different parts, in the ultimate sense there is no chariot (translated by Ñāṇamoli 1991: 612). This proposal is based on distinguishing between common parlance and what is real in the ultimate sense (*paramattha*). The resultant notion of two types of language or two types of truth is not found in the early discourses and can safely be considered a later development.

The simile of the chariot occurs in a discourse that involves a challenge by Māra (translated by Bodhi 2000: 230). As already mentioned in the first chapter (see p. 28), in several early discourses Māra functions as an impersonation of challenges, often those posed by outsiders to Buddhist practitioners (Anālayo 2015d: 201–5). The present instance is such a case, as Māra's challenge involves the implicit proposal of a substantialist view of a "living being." The wise *bhikkhunī* he has accosted is quick to dispel this notion. According to her explanation, the designation of a "living being" is similar to the designation of a "chariot," in that neither of the two implies the existence of a substantial entity. Instead, both living beings and chariots are assemblies of parts. This does not mean that there is no living being or no chariot. It means only that there is no substantial and permanent entity that can be referred to by these terms.

The *Visuddhimagga* conforms with this perspective when asserting that there is no living being in addition to or apart from the material and immaterial aggregates (translated by Ñāṇamoli 1991: 649). But elsewhere the same work argues that, in an ultimate sense, women and men do not exist (translated by Ñāṇamoli 1991: 535). Yet, women and men do exist as changing processes. The invoking of an ultimate sense can be confusing, as the teaching on not self does not intend to deny such impermanent and conditioned existence. The point is only that there is nothing permanent and stable in women or men.

Several passages show the Buddha reckoning himself to be foremost among "living beings" (translated by Bodhi 2000: 1550 and 2012: 421, 656, and 1354). This is not problematic at all, since in such contexts the term "living being" is not meant to convey the sense of some unchanging entity. The problem is not a particular term that has been employed. The problem rather lies in what this term is intended to convey.

The same can be seen in the formulation employed by a monastic upholding a mistaken view, which appears to imply the assumption that consciousness is an unchanging entity (translated by Ñāṇamoli 1995/2005: 349). Although in stating his view the monastic employed the term "consciousness," a term regularly used for the fifth aggregate, the implications it carried for him were clearly wrong. Just as the use of the term "living being" can be correctly employed, as long as it is divested from substantialist notions, so the use of the term "consciousness" can be incorrect, once it carries such notions. It is not the case that the former is ultimately nonexistent and the latter is ultimately real. What these two different terms designate is invariably conditioned and impermanent, devoid of an essence of its own.

A proper implementation of the teaching on not self does not require differentiating two types of language and considering any instance of a term like "living being" to be just common parlance (and implicitly not quite correct), whereas a term like "consciousness" is ultimate (and implicitly correct). Instead, it involves divesting all aspects of experience of any notion of there being a permanent entity, no matter what language is being used. The tendency toward reification cannot be solved by privileging one set of terms over another; in fact, the very act of privileging language can itself become a source for reification.

13. CLINGING AND AWAKENING

According to early Buddhist thought, the belief in some sort of a permanent entity will be left behind with stream entry, the first level of awakening. However, clinging to the five aggregates as "me" or "mine" will be overcome for good only with the attainment of the highest level of awakening. Once one has become an arahant, only the bare aggregates are left, and all clinging has been completely eradicated (Anālayo 2010a: 13–15).

In later tradition, this perspective on the gradual removal of types of clinging during successive stages of awakening has not always remained fully clear. A problem appears to have arisen due to a literal reading of the wording used in a Pāli discourse for describing four types of clinging (translated by Ñāṇamoli 1995/2005: 161). The Pāli version introduces one of these as involving clinging to a doctrine of self (*attavādupādāna*), whereas the parallel versions just speak of clinging to a self (Anālayo 2010a: 10–13 and 2011: 102–3).

Whereas clinging to a doctrine of self will be overcome already with stream entry, clinging to the subtle notion of a self will be left behind only with full awakening. If the fourth type of clinging concerns a "doctrine of a self," a problem arises in relation to the remaining three types of clinging: clinging to views, clinging to rules and observances, and clinging to sensual desires. The first two will be left behind with stream entry, whereas the third will be eradicated with the attainment of nonreturn, the third stage of awakening. The net result is that all types of clinging have already been abandoned with the third level of awakening and no form of clinging remains to be abandoned during the progress from non-return to becoming an arahant.

Buddhaghosa attempts to solve this problem by broadening his definition of the term *kāma*, used to refer to "sensual desire." The argument is that greed for fine-material and immaterial experiences should also be included under this heading (translated by Ñāṇamoli 1991: 711). Since such types of greed, related to the experience of the four absorptions and the four immaterial attainments, are left behind only with full awakening, in this way the gap can be closed by identifying a type of clinging to be eradicated during progress from nonreturn to full awakening. Yet, the standard definition of the first level of absorption in the discourses begins with an explicit reference to seclusion from all sensual desires as a precondition for its actual attainment. This precludes considering an absorption experience to be a possible object of sensual desire.

14. The Stages of Purification and Awakening

Theravāda exegesis considers the "path" and the "fruit" of nonreturn to be two mind moments that immediately follow each other (translated by Ñāṇamoli 1991: 701). In the early discourses, on the other hand, the notion of being on the path to any of the four levels of awakening can encompass a broad period of time (Anālayo 2012c: 77). The momentary perspective adopted in later tradition for all four levels of awakening does not sit well with early discourse references to those on the path and those who have reached the fruit.

This can be seen in an occurrence of such a listing in the context of a survey of recipients of offerings (translated by Ñāṇamoli 1995/2005: 1103). In its original formulation, the passage appears to have been about the merit accrued by giving to recipients who either have reached one of the levels of awakening or else are firmly on the path to one of these.

The corresponding commentary, however, reads the passage in the light of the idea that someone can be on the path to a level of awakening only for a moment and will right away after that turn into one who has reached that level. This then leads to the idea that the survey of recipients of offerings refers to awakening experiences taking place while being offered the meal. The original description, however, is quite probably not about awakenings attained while the meal offering is in progress.

The momentary perspective on the event of awakening features in the *Visuddhimagga* under the heading of "purification of knowledge and vision." This conforms with a basic scaffolding adopted in this work, taken from a discourse that describes seven stages of purification. These range from purification of virtue to purification of knowledge and vision (translated by Ñāṇamoli 1995/2005: 242).

A problem with adopting this scheme, however, is that in the original discourse the seven stages of purification do not cover the event of awakening. Instead, they only describe progress toward that goal. In fact, another discourse has a ninefold listing (translated by Walshe 1987: 519). Besides the seven already mentioned, this includes the purifications of wisdom and of deliverance. The last of these would have provided a better fit for the experience of awakening (Anālayo 2005: 133, 2009a: 9–11, and 2017b: 507n14).

The apparent error made in this way can be better appreciated on taking into account a work extant in Chinese that appears to have served as a model for the composition of the *Visuddhimagga*. This work, usually referred to by the Pāli title *Vimuttimagga*, the Path to Liberation, employs as its main scaffolding the four noble truths. In the course of its exposition, the *Vimuttimagga* also mentions four of the stages of purification (Anālayo 2009a: 8–11). This reference may have served as a starting point for Buddhaghosa to employ the full scheme of stages of purification, as a way of providing a more complete coverage than the *Vimuttimagga*. In the course of doing so, however, instead of adopting the nine stages of purification, he employed only the set of seven and thereby ended up including awakening under a heading that, in its original context, did not correspond to the consummation of the path (Ñāṇamoli 1991: 696).

According to traditional hagiography, however, rather than using the *Vimuttimagga* as his model, Buddhaghosa compiled the *Visuddhimagga*

Figure 9. Buddhaghosa and the three versions of the *Visuddhimagga*; Kelaniya.

entirely on his own. In fact, he did so thrice, as at the completion of the manuscript a celestial twice took it away, forcing him to start all over again (Law 1923: 36). When he had finished the third copy, the earlier two were returned to him and on inspection were found to be identical to the third one. Figure 9 shows Buddhaghosa and his three manuscripts, representing the three identical versions of the *Visuddhimagga* that, according to the traditional account, he had compiled independently of each other.

15. INSIGHT MEDITATION

Several of the shifts in understanding surveyed in the course of this chapter have influenced the teaching of *vipassanā* meditation. One of these is the notion of mindfulness as plunging into its objects, which can invest its cultivation with somewhat forceful nuances. According to U Paṇḍita (1992/1993: 99), for example, mindfulness "must be dynamic and confrontative. In retreats, I teach that mindfulness should leap forward onto the object."

Another aspect of perhaps even greater influence is the notion of momentariness, in the form of the belief that cultivating a direct experience of the moment-by-moment dissolution of all aspects of subjective experience is a necessary foundation for the progress of insight. This notion became central in the formation of *vipassanā* meditation, which emerged in the historical setting of colonial Myanmar. In order to fortify lay Buddhists against the influences of foreign domination and to ensure the longevity of Buddhism, Abhidharma teachings were made accessible to laity on a wide scale (Braun 2013). According to a prediction in Theravāda commentaries, the disappearance of the Abhidharma will herald the onset of the decline of Theravāda Buddhism (Endo 2004). In view of such apprehensions, an attempt to bolster tradition against the disintegrating influences of colonialism naturally tended to focus first of all on the preservation of the Abhidharma.

In this setting, insight meditation practice was taught alongside Abhidharma, mainly in order to lead to a direct experience of central tenets of Abhidharma thought. In other words, contemporary insight meditation teaching emerges as a byproduct of an attempt to fortify and strengthen a sense of Theravāda Buddhist identity. In this setting, a chief purpose of insight meditation practice was to lead to an experience of at least some of the ultimate realities recognized in the Theravāda exegetical tradition. By this time, a list of material and mental phenomena had been cataloged as being such ultimate realities, in line with the expansion of meaning of the fourth aggregate discussed earlier in this chapter. The task of mindfulness was to lead in particular to an experience of momentariness and the direct witnessing of the dissolution of mind and matter.

Contemporary insight meditation traditions facilitate such a direct experience of momentariness by encouraging a fragmentation of experience, breaking it down into its various components. Slow-motion walking can help to separate the apparent continuity of walking into discrete parts. Labeling of anything experienced serves to foster a realization of the immediate disappearance of whatever has just been noticed. Alternatively, repeated body scanning can lead to an experience of the energetic constitution of the body as a mass of vibrations in constant disintegration. Whatever approach is chosen, a chief task of insight meditation remains to lead to the insight knowledge of dissolution (*bhaṅga-ñāṇa*), which precedes the insight knowledge of fear. Directly and personally witnessing the dissolution of mind and matter serves to testify to the truth of the doctrine of momentariness, often based on a confrontational deployment of mindfulness as a quality that plunges into its objects.

16. ABSORPTION

Another aspect of the teaching of *vipassanā* meditation relates to concentration. A stream enterer is endowed with the factors of the noble eightfold path (translated by Bodhi 2000: 1793), including right concentration. Since one type of definition of "right concentration" lists the four absorptions (*jhāna*), this can give the impression that absorptive abilities are required for reaching even the first level of awakening.

The question of the supposed necessity of absorptive abilities for stream entry became a major controversy with the large-scale spread of *vipassanā* meditation. The type of *vipassanā* meditation taught by Mahāsi Sayādaw does not allocate time to the formal cultivation of mental tranquility. This left considerable room for criticism. Ostensibly as a way to forestall further criticism, Mahāsi Sayādaw and his disciples baptized experiences of insight meditation as a form of absorption, presented as being a "*vipassanā-jhāna*" (Anālayo 2020a).

This apparently polemical move appears to have set a precedent for a reinterpretation of the significance of absorption among Theravāda meditation practitioners, even leading to the idea that absorption in itself is productive of insight (Arbel 2017). Such an assumption is not an accurate reflection of the nature and purpose of absorption attainment described in the early discourses (Anālayo 2017c: 109–23 and 2020a).

Another related strand of reinterpretation takes the term *jhāna*, "absorption," to refer to experiences within easy reach of any practitioner, rather than requiring a high level of meditative expertise. Such assumptions also stand in contrast to the indications that can be gleaned from the early discourses, where the attainment of absorption appears to correspond to profound concentrative experiences that require considerable meditative training (Anālayo 2017c: 123–50 and 2019j).

A case in point is a description of the Buddha's own prolonged struggle with various obstructions to the attainment of the first absorption, which he related to his monastic disciple Anuruddha, who had similar problems (translated by Ñāṇamoli 1995/2005: 1012). Anuruddha features in the list of eminent monastic disciples as outstanding for clairvoyance, which requires a high degree of concentrative ability. Another discourse reports that the Buddha's own eventual mastery of absorption was such that he was able to enter each of these at will in ascending and descending order even while being on the verge of passing away (translated by Walshe 1987: 271 and Bodhi 2000: 251). For the Buddha and this outstanding disciple to have to struggle initially to attain and stabilize even just the first absorption, in spite of their evident abilities attested by their later meditative mastery, makes it fairly obvious that in the thought-world of the early discourses the term *jhāna* indeed stood for profound meditative experiences.

Besides, a comparative study of references to "right concentration" in the early discourses brings to light that an equation with the attainment of the four absorptions does not seem to reflect the earliest stages in defining this particular path factor (Anālayo 2019b). The original idea of what makes concentration "right" appears to have been rather the need to cultivate it in collaboration with the other seven path factors. Of particular importance here is right view. In fact, mere attainment of absorption in the absence of right view would hardly qualify as being the path factor of right concentration.

This in turn makes it fair to conclude that the attainment of stream entry does not require the cultivation of absorptive abilities. In fact, some reports of stream entry attainment in Pāli discourses involve persons who may not have meditated at all previously, let alone been proficient in absorption (Anālayo 2003: 80). From this viewpoint, there would have been no need to invent "*vipassanā-jhānas*," with its apparent repercussions to fuel attempts to authenticate lightly concentrated meditation experiences by applying to them the prestigious label of *jhāna*.

SUMMARY

The conservatism characteristic of Theravādins may be the result of specific historical circumstances and does not justify a claim to being the sole nonschismatic Buddhist tradition and the only representative of original Buddhism. Comparative study shows that Pāli discourses are just as prone to reflect later ideas as are discourses of other transmission lineages. Hence, the notion that the Pāli canon is the only true repository of the original teachings of the Buddha is not tenable.

As the sacred language of Theravāda Buddhism, Pāli has come to be imbued with an aura of intrinsic extraordinariness that is not quite in keeping with the early Buddhist attitude toward language. A preoccupation with the correct pronunciation of Pāli ordination formulae, for example, reflects an attitude inherited from the Vedic traditions rather than from the historical Buddha.

The Theravāda tradition has embraced the bodhisattva ideal as a viable option for practice, alongside the normative goal of becoming an arahant. Buddhaghosa himself aspired to be reborn at the time of the future Buddha Maitreya, rather than desiring to become an arahant as soon as possible.

Another later notion is the belief that the Buddha was omniscient, which appears to have become a central driving force in the evolution of Abhidharma thought. Eventually considered to be the supreme representation of Buddhist thought, Theravādins utilized modes of authentication of Abhidharma scripture similar to those in use by followers of the Mahāyāna for their texts.

In line with the drive for comprehensiveness characteristic of Abhidharma thought, the compass of the fourth aggregate expanded from its core meaning of volitional formations to embracing a vast assembly of mental factors and qualities. One of the qualities included under this header is mindfulness. Due to an apparent error or reinterpretation of a particular Pāli term, mindfulness came to be invested with the quality of plunging into its object. This notion has been of considerable influence in the spread of Theravāda *vipassanā* meditation.

Comparable to the shift in understanding of the quality of mindfulness, the employment of this quality for meditation on the breath also underwent change. Whereas relevant instructions in the early discourses come with an emphasis on joy and happiness as factors leading to concentration, in later times an emphasis on the breath alone was combined with the method of counting the breaths.

A comparable change in meditation practice can be seen in the case of the divine abodes, whose boundless radiation is regularly described in the early discourses. According to the traditional Theravāda approach to this practice, however, during meditation the divine abodes are to be directed to individual persons, and the radiation becomes relevant only once the practitioner has developed this person-oriented approach up to the level of being able to attain absorption.

In the early texts, the key idea behind the teaching on dependent arising appears to have been the principle of specific conditionality, which the oft-found list of twelve links illustrates. In Theravāda exegesis, however, the significance of this principle becomes to some degree buried under details, when each of the links of dependent arising is approached by relying on an additional scheme of twenty-four conditions.

A significant shift from early Buddhist thought, shared by a range of Buddhist traditions, is the evolution of the theory of momentariness. As a result of this development, the continuity of phenomena as changing processes came to be effaced in favor of the idea that everything will immediately disappear after having arisen.

The notion that experiences of fear reflect an advanced stage in the progress of insight is not found in the early discourses and only becomes prominent in later Theravāda exegesis. The standard translation of *dukkha* as "suffering" conflates the reaction of an untrained mind with a characteristic applicable to all conditioned phenomena.

Interpreting the teaching on not self appears to have led to statements that have their underpinning in the notion of two types of language or truth, one expressing common convention, the other carrying an ultimate sense. This notion is absent from early Buddhist thought, where the doctrine of not self stands for the absence of a permanent entity, rather than implying that there is nothing at all.

A term used in Pāli discourses to describe a particular type of clinging seems to have created problems in correlating the removal of different types of clinging with progress through successive levels of awakening, leading to a broadening of the compass of the term "sensual desire" in Theravāda exegesis.

Theravāda exegetical literature approaches the progress to awakening from a momentary perspective, according to which being on the "path" lasts for a moment only and is right away followed by realizing the corresponding "fruit." In the early discourses, however, being on the path can cover a much longer span of time.

When depicting the progress to awakening, Buddhaghosa relied on stages of purification described in the discourses. Due to an apparent blunder, he correlated the completion of such progress with the seventh stage of purification, whose implication in its original setting falls short of covering the actual event of awakening.

Contemporary insight meditation appears to have originated from an attempt to fortify lay Buddhist disciples against the disintegrating influences of Western colonialism. This attempt had as its main concern the inculcation of Abhidharma teachings, with insight meditation emerging as a convenient means to lead to a direct experience of the truth of these teachings. In this setting, momentariness naturally emerged as a central concern of insight meditation, in combination with the Theravādin notion of mindfulness as a quality that plunges into its objects.

In an apparent attempt to counter criticism for not dedicating time and practice to the cultivation of absorptive concentration, pioneers in the spread of *vipassanā* meditation resorted to the move of referring to experiences of insight meditation as a form of *jhāna*. The idea resulting from the need to counter such criticism took on its own dynamics and began to influence practitioners interested in cultivating deeper levels of concentration. In this setting, it eventually appears to have inspired either alleging that absorption attainment is in itself productive of liberating insight and awakening, or else assuming that even lightly concentrated states of mind can be invested with the prestigious label *jhāna* and thereby be authenticated.

The Theravāda insight meditation traditions that have evolved based on ideas surveyed above have successfully spread around the world and have helped many to gain liberating insight and stages of awakening. Even though this has taken place based on ideas that differ from teachings in the early discourses, what counts in the end is that practitioners have benefitted. This is indubitably the case.

Even the reinterpretation of the term *jhāna* to include experiences within fairly easy reach has its practical benefits. It has helped to counterbalance the emphasis on dry insight in *vipassanā* traditions by encouraging an intentional cultivation of factors of absorption, in particular joy and happiness.

In sum, the developments surveyed above can have quite beneficial results and the *Visuddhimagga* has much to offer for meditation practice. In fact, even Buddhaghosa's apparent error in correlating awakening with the seventh purification is, after all, simply a matter of presentation, without further significance. The positive contributions made in his work have not been taken up more explicitly here because they fall outside of the scope of this chapter. The main point to be taken away from the above survey is thus simply that the superiority conceit of some Theravādins as being the sole custodians of the Buddha's original teachings is unfounded.

IV. Secular Buddhism

INTRODUCTION

MY LAST AREA of exploration in this book is Secular Buddhism, which at times comes with the conceit of superiority over other Buddhist traditions. Just as in the last chapter I focused on Buddhaghosa and his work at exemplifying trends in Theravāda exegesis, in the present chapter I focus on Stephen Batchelor as the foundational proponent of Secular Buddhism. In both cases such focus is simply an expedient for exploring the respective topic and does not imply that these two authors are the sole advocates of the ideas studied. Another similarity is that in both cases the main thrust of my exploration is to try to ascertain to what extent certain ideas reflect early Buddhist thought, given that both Buddhaghosa and Stephen Batchelor operate from the implicit or explicit position of accurately representing the teachings of the historical Buddha. In both cases, I take up only selected points without any pretense at providing a comprehensive coverage of their respective works.

In the case of Stephen Batchelor's formulation of Secular Buddhism in particular, the question at stake is not whether a particular idea is appealing in current times. Nor does my presentation in any way attempt to curtail his personal freedom to uphold certain views or to consider himself to be a Buddhist. The question is simply whether such views and ideas are supported by the sources that reflect early Buddhist thought.

After a brief look at the colonial heritage influencing Western perceptions of Asian Buddhists, I take up the notion of the construction of Buddhism, the question of whether early Buddhism is an -ism, and the contrast between lay and monastic practitioners. Then I turn to the significance of the Buddha as an "Awakened One," the nature of awakening, and Nirvana. After a brief look at the topic of rebirth, I explore the teaching of the four noble truths and the notion of truth as such. The points that emerge in the course of my survey lead me to evaluate Stephen Batchelor's writings from the viewpoint of their underlying methodology.

1. THE COLONIAL HERITAGE

By way of providing a background to Western Buddhism in general and Secular Buddhism in particular, I begin with a brief survey of selected aspects of the colonial heritage that inevitably has influenced Western perceptions of Asian Buddhists and their practices. Since Western knowledge about Buddhism has its starting point and foundation in the information gathered by Christian missionaries, my particular interest here is in strategies employed during the colonial period by such missionaries in their attempts to convert Asian Buddhists. The present brief survey is not intended to be comprehensive or even to imply that the selected voices are representative of the attitudes held by the majority of Christian missionaries. Instead, what follows is merely an assembly of a few strands that can be helpful for appreciating certain trends and attitudes among Western Buddhists.

Harris (2006: 85) notes as one relevant strategy the tendency of "representing Buddhism in practice as antiquated, static, rather romantic and in need of new energy from modern developments." The evaluation of the Buddhist doctrine of rebirth by some Christian missionaries can in turn be exemplified with the assessment that "transmigration is ridiculous to the reasoning mind" (Harris 2006: 50). In an attempt to dichotomize the supposedly true teachings of the Buddha from their imperfect practice by living Buddhists, a Christian missionary strategy was to contrast the teaching of not self with belief in rebirth (Young and Somaratna 1996: 82–83). Such a contrast rests on the (mistaken) assumption that rebirth must involve some form of a soul that is reborn and hence is incompatible with the denial of the existence of such a soul in Buddhist doctrine.

The contrast drawn in this way naturally lends itself to the reasoning that "Buddhist cosmology and narratives about the 'incarnations', or previous lives, of the Buddha are 'an interminable labyrinth of absurdities'" (Harris 2006: 78). According to Young and Somaratna (1996: 97), one prong in a particular instance of sustained theistic critique of Buddhism was the attempt "to rupture the confidence of Sinhalese Buddhists in *karma* as a construct capable of accounting for the contrarieties in human existence in the absence of a God." Harris (2006: 56) adds that "some missionaries combined nihilist interpretations of *nibbāna* and the Buddhist religious life with the trivializing of rebirth."

A related trend is evident in a missionary book written for children, which according to Harris (2006: 106) had the clear aim "to place the Buddha firmly in the realm of the mundane." In relation to another book compiled by a Christian missionary, Harris (2006: 68) reports that

> the aim of the book is to ridicule the trustworthiness of the Buddha's teachings by comparing them with Western science. Reducing the Buddha's enlightenment to the non-mystical event of an ardent, young, spiritual seeker coming to the wrong conclusions feeds into this.

A strongly dismissive attitude toward Buddhism can be seen in a Christian hymn, written in 1840 for the Anniversary of the Ceylon Baptist Mission (Harris 2006: 60–61), which contains the following verses:

> Buddha's shrines are fast-forsaken,
> Crumbles many an Idol fane!
> Slumb'rers have begun to waken
> And to find all refuge vain . . .
> Strengthen every Christian warrior
> Make the powers of darkness fall;
> Cast down each opposing barrier,
> Now, at length, the heathen call,
> Reign victorious,
> God! Redeemer! all in all!

In sum, strategies adopted by some Christian missionaries for the sake of converting Asian Buddhists are the allegation that the teachings on rebirth are self-contradictory, based on the assumption that stories of previous lives, etc., are unrelated to the true doctrines of Buddhism, which in its actual practice is anyway antiquated and in need of renewal. A dismissal of Nirvana goes hand in hand with a reduction of the significance of the Buddha's awakening and an attempt to place him firmly in the mundane sphere, under the overarching hope that Buddhists will find their three refuges vain and thereby be inspired to convert to Christianity. I will return to these strategies toward the end of this chapter.

2. The Construction of Buddhism

Terms like "Buddhism" and "Theravāda" have at times been considered to be merely the result of Western influence. Although often meant to alert the public to the agenda of Western colonial powers in constructing a coherent narrative of the colonized, such suggestions run the risk of depriving Asians of agency and of turning a blind eye to comparable notions and precedents already found in the respective indigenous traditions well before the colonial period. As pointed out by Bretfeld (2012: 275) in a different context,

> we have to be cautious that the rhetoric of "construction" and "invention" does not draw our attention only to the historical breaks or make us lose sight of the continuities as well as the amount of Asian agency and traditional resources involved in these processes.

Regarding the term "Theravāda," already taken up briefly in the previous chapter (see p. 76), Perreira (2012: 554) argued that a British man who had become a Theravāda monk at the beginning of the twentieth century in Burma "was himself the source of our modern use of 'Theravāda'—and not a Burmese text or Burmese informant." Closer inspection shows the situation to be considerably more complex, as Asian antecedents to such usage can be identified (Anālayo 2016a: 508–10).

A more frequently made claim of this type concerns the term "Buddhism" itself. An example is the suggestion by Batchelor (2015: 17) that, like other modern terms that lack Buddhist equivalents, the same holds for "the very word 'Buddhism,' a term coined by Western scholars in the nineteenth century, which also has no equivalent in Pali, Sanskrit, Chinese, or Tibetan." Here, too, the situation appears to be considerably more complex.

Needless to say, that the English term itself is not found in an area and a time when no English was spoken is obvious and does not carry further significance. The question at stake is thus not the English term "Buddhism," but much rather whether equivalents to this term in Buddhist languages were in existence before the nineteenth century.

An apparent antecedent to the concept of Buddhism could be found in the term *buddhasāsana*, which nowadays can function as an equivalent to Buddhism in Theravāda countries. As is the case with the term *theravāda*, this term occurs already in the Pāli discourses, where it usually carries the sense of the teaching or the dispensation of the historical Buddha Gotama.

An example is a verse which speaks of a young monastic who joins or applies himself to the *buddhasāsana*. Found in the *Dhammapada* collection (382), the verse has parallels in Chinese, Sanskrit, and Tibetan (Anālayo 2011: 499n290). Three of the four Chinese parallels render the expression *buddhasāsana* with precisely the term that in modern Chinese translates Buddhism: *fojiao* (Taishō numbers 210, 211, and 212). The earliest of these three translations dates to the first part of the third century of the present era and thus to an initial period in Buddhist translation activities in China. Already at that time, a Chinese equivalent to the term Buddhism was evidently in use. It remains to be seen how far the corresponding Pāli term conveys the sense of a distinct religious tradition.

Another two verses in the *Dhammapada* collection (183 and 185) speak of the *sāsana* of Buddhas (plural). As the context concerns what is common to the teachings given by Buddhas of the past, present, and future, it goes beyond the notion of what was specifically taught by the historical Buddha Gotama.

A verse in the *Theragāthā* (181) speaks of going forth in the *buddhasāsana*, in the sense of ordaining as a Buddhist monastic. This already conveys a sense that goes beyond just a type of teaching. The nuance of a Buddhist tradition emerges more pronouncedly in the *Milindapañha*, a text datable to a few centuries after the time of the Buddha. The relevant part of the work considers the *buddhasāsana* to be under threat of dissolution, the avoidance of which requires converting the Bactrian Greek king Milinda (translated by Horner 1969: 11 and 19). In a context concerned with conversion, the term *buddhasāsana* does convey a more distinct sense of a religious tradition.

Such a sense becomes still more conspicuous in an occurrence of just the term *sāsana*, which here is obviously the Buddha's *sāsana*, found in a Sri Lankan chronicle from about the fifth century. The occurrence concerns the expulsion from Sri Lanka of the Tamil army, who had earlier invaded the country from South India. Such an expulsion is said to bring glory to the *sāsana* (translated by Geiger 1912: 170). The usage in this chronicle no longer accommodates the notion of a "teaching." In fact, bringing glory to the *sāsana* in this way resulted in a considerable number of killings.

Killing other human beings in battle stands in contrast to the first precept and to the Buddha's explicit depiction of the negative karmic consequences of engaging in warfare (Anālayo 2009b). Whereas in the *Milindapañha* the question was only conversion, here the issue is about going to war for the sake of the Buddha's *sāsana*. Carter (1993: 15) comments that "*sāsana* had, by this time, acquired a broader, reified, indeed, institutional meaning."

It seems fair to conclude that the word "Buddhism" has counterparts in ancient Buddhist languages, such as Pāli and Chinese, and its meaning as a distinct religious tradition that requires conversion and being defended in war had emerged long before the nineteenth century.

The assumption that the term "Buddhism" is a creation of the nineteenth century has already been criticized by von Hinüber (2002: 267), who notes that taking such a position "does not do justice to Indian literature, where 'Buddhism' as a concept was always present," citing as an example a drama from the eleventh century.

Indian inscriptions voicing antagonistic attitudes toward Buddhists from the eleventh and twelfth centuries reflect the same sense. According to the translations provided by Verardi (2018: 276, 430, and 438), some

Figure 10. Bhairava Dancing on the Severed Heads
of Buddhist Monks; probably Orissa.

such inscriptions refer to overcoming "the crowds of Bauddhas," drying up the "Bauddha doctrine," and destroying the "Bauddha religion." The hostility evident in these inscriptions can also be seen in a depiction from the same period shown in figure 10, in which the four-armed Hindu god Bhairava plays music and dances on five severed heads of Buddhist monks. Such sentiments clearly reflect a perception of Buddhism as a religious tradition that needs to be vanquished. These examples can be seen as a counterpart to the notion, evident in a fifth-century Sri Lanka chronicle, that fighting against the Tamil army will bring glory to the Buddhist dispensation. Taken together, they point to the existence of the notion of *Buddhism* from both an emic and an etic perspective.

Turning from Asia to the West, Batchelor (1994: 28) considers the first mention of the Buddha in European literature to be a reference given by the Church Father Clement of Alexandria, who lived in the second century after the present era. According to Clement's report, some Indians followed the precepts of the Buddha (*Stromata* I.15; Heinsius 1616: 223). The actual reference employs the Greek noun *parangélma*, with its Latin equivalent in *praeceptum*, which conveys the idea of "precepts." This seems to correspond to the idea of taking precepts in the Buddhist tradition, which could be either as a lay follower or else as a Buddhist monastic. Such parallelism would imply that already Clement of Alexandria had some idea of followers of the Buddha as belonging to a distinct religious tradition, with the adoption of precepts functioning as an expression of membership.

This in turn entails that even the Western construction of Buddhism began much earlier than the nineteenth century. When Batchelor (1994: 227) introduces Eugène Burnouf under the header of "the construction of Buddhism," then this is correct only insofar as the eminent nineteenth-century French scholar gave coherence and depth to the bits and pieces of Western knowledge of the Buddhist traditions. But the various forms of Buddhism in Asia are of course quite independent of what Westerners knew or did not know about them, just as the Americas did not come into being only since the time of Columbus.

The perception of Buddhism as a tradition comprising more than disparate local traditions is also evident in the example of Sri Lankan *bhikkhunīs* travelling to China, mentioned in the first chapter (see p. 9). For women in those days to undertake such a journey to an unknown country with totally different customs and language is nothing short of heroic. In fact, two *bhikkhunīs* died on the way and another group of *bhikkhunīs* had to be brought from Sri Lanka to fulfill the quorum required for granting ordination to the Chinese. The motivation of the Sri Lanka *bhikkhunīs* to undertake such journeys must have been grounded in a sense of Buddhist fellowship, based on a perception of Buddhism as a religious tradition that goes beyond the confines of local groups of practitioners.

The above survey does not intend to propose that the term "Buddhism" stands for some monolithic entity inherent in the diverse Buddhist traditions in existence in the past or at present. Any concept descriptive of a social and historical reality invariably has to comprise variety under a single term. Such limitations of concepts apply to "Buddhism" just as much as to "Europe" or "Western," for example, as these terms could also be misunderstood to refer to something monolithic. In line with a point made in the previous chapter in relation to the doctrine of not self, the issue is not a particular term per se, but what it is taken to imply (see p. 93). The potential for the term "Buddhism" to be mistaken as implying a monolithic entity is not a problem specific to this term but is much rather a problem of the limitations inherent in descriptive concepts in general.

3. Buddh-ism

A related question is to what degree the sources reflecting the early period of Buddhism convey the sense of an -ism. According to Batchelor (1997: 17), "first and foremost the Buddha taught a method ("dharma *practice*") rather than another '-ism'. The dharma is not something to believe in but something to do."

Concerning the suggestion that the Dharma is not something to believe in, of relevance are the five spiritual faculties (*indriya*) or powers (*bala*) that are a key element in the Buddhist conception of the path, and hence are directly about what "to do." The first of these is trust or confidence (*saddhā*). Gethin (2016: 185) explains that

> Buddhist texts understand faith in the Buddha, Dharma and Sangha not so much as a question of belief that certain propositions about the world are true, [but] as a state of trust, . . . a confidence that there is indeed a path leading to the cessation of suffering which has been walked by the Buddha and at least some of his followers.

In order to embark on the "to do" part of the teachings, there is a need first of all to generate confidence in the Buddha's awakening and in his having indeed discovered the path to full awakening (Anālayo 2017f: 227). This requires initially taking on trust what for the time being is beyond one's personal, direct verification.

Regarding the question of whether Buddhism is an -ism in the sense of an institutionalized sense of identity, a relevant passage would be the report in the Pāli *Vinaya* that the Buddha regulated how the robes worn by his monastic disciples should be made (translated by Horner 1938/1982: 408). The same is recorded in other *Vinayas* as well, several of which introduce the regulation with a narrative. According to this narrative, a local king had venerated the followers of another tradition, mistaking them for Buddhist monastics (Frauwallner 1956: 98). The regulation served to forestall this happening again. From this viewpoint, the designing of robes that made Buddhist monastics easily recognizable points to an attempt to promote some degree of institutional identity.

The sense of an institutional identity also emerges in passages found among the discourses that refer to a special probation period required of those who wished to join the Buddhist monastic order but had previously been members of another tradition (e.g. Anālayo 2011: 397n46). Such a procedure does not seem to have been considered necessary if a layman wished to join the monastic order. In fact, some degree of "othering" is a recurrent feature in the early discourses, with relevant instances conveying a distinct sense of demarcating monastic disciples of the Buddha from non-Buddhist wanderers (Freiberger 2000: 58–71 and 99–108).

Even the conversion of lay disciples concerns institutional allegiance, with potential economic repercussions. A case in point is the conversion of a wealthy lay follower of the Jains, leading to the Buddha recommending that his newly won disciple should still continue offering food to Jain mendicants (Anālayo 2011: 327). Alongside showing the Buddha's magnanimous attitude, the episode also reflects the competition in the ancient Indian setting between different mendicant orders vying for lay support. For such competition to exist, the Jain and Buddhist monastic orders had to have identifiable institutional identities.

According to the Pāli canonical account of his decease, when close to passing away the Buddha informed a wanderer (who was to become his last convert) that the stages of awakening could be found only in a dispensation that had the eightfold path (translated by Walshe 1987: 268). Most parallel versions agree with the Pāli discourse in reporting this statement; the one version that diverges nevertheless expresses the uniqueness of the Buddha's teaching in a complementary manner (Waldschmidt 1948: 227–31). The same assessment of the distinctiveness of the Buddha's dispensation recurs in another discourse (translated by Ñāṇamoli 1995: 159). Although in this case the parallels differ in the degree to which they give prominence to this statement, they agree on its basic sense (Anālayo 2016a: 45–49).

These few passages suffice to show that the early texts do reflect a sense of an institutionalized identity, both in the sense of uniqueness among other ancient Indian practitioners in terms of spiritual attainment and by way of an intentional employment of outer markers to convey this sense of identity to others. This would have to be considered as reflecting a form of "-ism," in the sense of a corporate identity that goes beyond merely teaching others what to do.

4. Monasticism

In line with a general tendency among Secular Buddhists of extolling lay practice and being at times somewhat dismissive about monasticism, Batchelor (2015: 47) apparently considers Buddhist monasticism to be a later development, coming into being only in

> a later period in Buddhist history, when mendicants came to live apart in monasteries, functioned as priests, and depended on the laity to provide not only daily almsfood but the upkeep and protection of their institutions.

Batchelor (2015: 14) therefore sees a need "to recover the kind of egalitarian community that the Buddha envisioned." Not only that, but Batchelor (2017: 131) even proposes that "insistence on monasticism as central to the survival of Buddhism could hasten its downfall rather than ensure its preservation."

The belief that Buddhist monasticism is a later development is an outdated opinion, originating in part from a misinterpretation of the solitary life depicted in the Discourse on the Rhinoceros as normative for Indian

Buddhist monastics in general (Anālayo 2017i: 101–5). As noted by Collins (1990: xvi–xvii),

> to accept the myth of a transition 'from eremitical to cenobitical life' is, as the Christian terminology shows, to impose on Buddhist monastic history categories derived from the received wisdom about Christian tradition—which is itself equally legendary and unhistorical . . . the evidence shows that the ideal system of monasticism . . . is, in general, a single and coherent one; we are not presented with a series of historical layers and an evolution from one thing to another.

The idea that the Buddha envisioned an egalitarian community does not reflect the early texts particularly well. For example, a discourse reports the Buddha quite explicitly stating that he considered his monastic disciples to be superior and more worthy of his attention than his lay disciples (translated by Bodhi 2000: 1339). This finds illustration in two similes, which compare the monastic disciples to an excellent field for farming and to a watertight pot for storing water, whereas the lay disciples are similar to a field of middling quality and a pot that is not watertight. The point made by the simile is that a farmer will first sow seeds in the excellent field and store water in the watertight pots, just as the Buddha will give precedence to monastic disciples over lay disciples when dispensing his teachings.

This is hardly a vision of an egalitarian community. Such a suggestion appears to confuse soteriological inclusiveness with social hierarchy, projecting a notion of egalitarianism, fashionable in contemporary secular circles, onto early Buddhism. As explained by Sponberg (1997: 352),

> While it is certainly true that Buddhism advocated, in its early form at least, a . . . decentralized institutional structure, this should not be misconstrued in the light of our current Western concerns to mean that the spiritual ideal in Buddhism was seen as nonhierarchical and egalitarian.

The proposal that insistence on the centrality of monasticism could lead to the downfall of Buddhism stands in direct contrast to the role accorded to the monastic order in early Buddhism. The act of becoming a Buddhist involves taking three refuges, the third of which is the monastic Saṅgha. This differs from the Saṅgha as an object of meditative recollection, which instead concerns those at various stages on the path to awakening, lay or monastic (Anālayo 2017i: 171). But the taking of refuge, in the way this is phrased in early Buddhist texts, takes as its object the monastic Saṅgha (*bhikkhusaṅgha*). From the perspective of early Buddhism, far from causing a downfall, the three refuges that ensure the preservation of Buddhism are the Buddha (who of course lived the life of a monastic himself), his teachings, and the community of his *monastic* disciples.

According to another reasoning by Batchelor (2015: 89), "in comparing the aim of his teaching to the rebuilding of an ancient city, the Buddha presents his goal as something entirely secular." Closer inspection shows the central element in the parable of the ancient city to be the Buddha's discovery of the path to awakening and not a vision of the goal as something secular. The idea of rebuilding the ancient city, supposedly conveying a secular orientation, is not taken up when the implications of the parable are drawn out and therefore is clearly a secondary element of the depiction (translated by Bodhi 2000: 603). It is hardly convincing to take such a secondary aspect of a particular simile out of its context and use that to propose an interpretation that contrasts with what the majority of other early discourses convey. Instead of the rebuilding of a city, the path is the key element in the comparison and this indeed reflects a central concern of the early Buddhist teachings, mentioned time and again in the discourses.

5. The Buddha

In early Buddhist thought, the goal attained by the Buddha and his arahant followers is the extinction of the three root defilements of greed, anger, and delusion, which could hardly be construed as a secular goal comparable to rebuilding a city. Another regular expression for the same accomplishment refers to the influxes (*āsavas*) of sensuality, becoming, and ignorance, which are completely eradicated once awakening has been attained. Batchelor (2015: 63), however, argues that

> Gotama's awakening is said to have involved the "stilling" and "fading away" of these reactive forces and drives. But if such instincts are neurobiological functions of our organism, it is difficult to understand how they can be systematically overcome—"cut off like a palm stump," as many discourses claim, "never to arise again." Although Buddhist orthodoxy insists that these forces and drives have been eliminated in arahants and buddhas, another, less prominent thread in the canon offers a more intelligible account of the ceasing of reactivity.

This less prominent but more intelligible account relates to Māra, whom Batchelor (2014: 20 and 28) considers to be "a metaphoric way of describing Buddha's own inner life," in the sense that Māra "is really Gotama's own conflicted humanity." On this premise, Batchelor (2015: 308–9) then reasons that

> a central paradox in the life of Gotama is that of a man who famously conquered the forces of Māra on the night of the awakening only to continue for the remaining forty-five years of his life to have intimate dealings with the very same forces. Clearly, then, he did not successfully delete reactivity from his experience; it was not, as the discourses say, "cut off like a palm stump, never to arise again" ... [Moreover], from the perspective of modern biology, greed and hatred are a legacy of our evolutionary past. They are physical drives rooted in our limbic system ... [hence] it seems naïve to think that meditation could permanently delete them from our limbic system. Their force may be diminished by not acting on them, but their underlying presence will persist. This scientific perspective helps us understand how Gotama conquered Māra by no longer assenting to him but was still subject to Māra's promptings.

The idea that greed and hatred are an inevitable heritage of evolution and can never be overcome does not appear to be a "scientific perspective," as to the best of my knowledge this has not been proven in any scientific research. In fact, Stephen Batchelor does not refer to relevant literature that would substantiate this claim.

This in turn implies that his position rests mainly on the proposed interpretation of Māra. This interpretation, however, does not accurately reflect the role and significance of Māra in early Buddhist texts. The various episodes involving Māra, reported in these texts, are not invariably reflections of inner uncertainties or defilements of the person he accosts. The figure of Māra can equally well serve to personify ancient Indian attitudes of derision and contempt, and even threat, toward Buddhists (Anālayo 2015d: 201–5). As already mentioned in the first chapter (see p. 28), by having Māra personify threats posed by outsiders, the respective teaching can show to the audience how such challenges are best dealt with. Moreover, providing the interpretative tool of viewing any actual threat as the work of Māra inculcates the proper attitude of mental balance and makes it easier to avoid reacting to it.

A case in point is the episode, mentioned in the first chapter, where Māra accosts an awakened *bhikkhunī* with the challenge of women's supposed inability to reach the status of a sage (see p. 28). This description is not about giving Māra the role of acting out some inner uncertainties of the *bhikkhunī* in question. Instead, this episode shows how to face such biases, typical of the patriarchal setting in ancient India, through the exemplary way in which the *bhikkhunī* responds.

The famous attack of Māra and his army on the eve of the Buddha's awakening (translated by Jayawickrama 1990: 95–98), depicted in figure 11, might indeed be read as a metaphorical way of describing inner struggles. However, this is a later hagiographical tale not found in the early discourses. For this reason, it cannot be taken as the normative representation of the function and role of Māra in the early texts.

A proper appreciation of the function of Māra in early Buddhist discourse makes it clear that his encounters with the Buddha do not reflect the latter's inner uncertainties. Instead, they depict how a fully awakened one faces challenges posed by others.

Figure 11. The Victory over Māra and His Host, on the
Eve of Awakening; Dunhuang (now Musée Guimet).

The idea that the Buddha had not completely eradicated the influxes
stands in stark contrast to a range of early Buddhist texts. One example
out of many is the second of his four intrepidities (Anālayo 2011: 109).
This concerns his absolute certainty that he had indeed completely eradicated the influxes. Whatever may be one's personal belief regarding the
possibility of achieving complete freedom from greed and anger, the texts
reflecting early Buddhist thought indubitably consider such freedom to
have been reached by the Buddha and large numbers of his followers.

6. AWAKENING

Regarding the Buddha's awakening, Batchelor (2017: 95) also does not consider it to have occurred at a particular point in time. According to his understanding, "awakening is not a singular insight . . . but a complex sequence of interrelated achievements gained through reconfiguring one's core relationship with *dukkha*." Hence, Batchelor (2015: 65) finds it likely that the Buddha's awakening "occurred gradually over many years of studying, learning, reflecting, discussing, arguing, and meditating." In line with his belief that defilements are an inevitable part of being human, Batchelor (2015: 74) then reasons about

> guilt, self-doubt, vanity, inadequacy, anxiety, conceit, para-
> noia, expectation, wishful thinking, and so on. Such reactions
> are entirely natural. They are neither good nor bad. . . . They
> are simply what happens when an organism interacts with its
> environment.

Once awakening is no longer a matter of overcoming defilements, and states considered in early Buddhism as unwholesome come to be seen as neither good nor bad, the role of ethics also changes. Batchelor (2015: 86) proposes that already with stream entry, the first level of awakening, one in a way goes beyond the felt need to adhere to moral codes, which tend

> to be based in the assumption that bad actions have a certain
> intrinsic nature whereas good actions have a quite different
> nature. Those who are moral, therefore, follow the rules laid
> out in this code with the complacent assurance of knowing
> they are "right." But those who have entered the stream of the
> path have become "independent of others." Not being tied to a
> code of conduct devised by others, they will respond in unpre-
> dictable ways to whatever moral dilemmas they encounter.

Regarding the first of these suggestions, made about the early Buddhist notion of awakening, a discourse can be consulted which lists three events worth being remembered (translated by Bodhi 2012: 206). Comparable to a king who recalls where he was born, where he was crowned, and where he gained victory in battle, these three events are where one went forth into the monastic life, where one gained stream entry, and where one attained full awakening by completely eradicating the influxes. These three events are indubitably considered to happen at a specific time and place. Moreover, this discourse describes the third event worth remembering by referring to the destruction of the influxes. This confirms once more that, from the viewpoint of early Buddhist thought, defilements are indeed completely removed from the mind when full awakening is attained.

Turning to the distinction between what is wholesome or skillful (*kusala*) and its opposite, in early Buddhist thought this distinction is not to be left behind with awakening, and even arahant monastics follow the code of rules. In a telling story, found in the different *Vinaya*s, the Buddha encourages an arahant monastic to participate in the fortnightly recital of the code of rules, even though the monastic had nothing to confess (Frauwallner 1956: 79). The passage conveys the need to behave according to "a code of conduct devised by others" rather than responding in unpredictable ways.

The reference to being independent of others in the standard description of stream entry reflects the inner certainty of one who has had penetrative insight into the essence of the teachings. In the early discourses such becoming independent of others can lead to the decision to go forth as a monastic and thereby undertake the monastic precepts (e.g. translated by Walshe 1987: 216) or else to undertake the moral precepts for lay disciples (e.g. translated by Bodhi 2012: 1148). Such descriptions would hardly have come into existence, had the idea been that the independence gained with stream entry refers to leaving behind adherence to a moral code of conduct devised by others.

7. Nirvana

Prominent among some Secular Buddhists is a reinterpretation of the notion of Nirvana. In an earlier publication, Batchelor (1983: 45) still considered the early Buddhist view of Nirvana to be the "complete antithesis" to *saṃsāra*, pointing to a "completely other condition of freedom" beyond description and hence referred to as the "unborn, unaging, undecaying, undying, and unsorrowing." Over a decade later, however, for Batchelor (1997: 9–10) the unborn and undying has become an "infinitely creative dimension of life," which "no sooner it is glimpsed than it is gone. Cessation of craving is like a momentary gap in the clouds." By this time, Batchelor (1997: 102) had come to see the idea that Nirvana is an ultimate release from *saṃsāra* to be analogous to taking alcohol and opiates, as "such self-abnegation would deny a central element of our humanity: the need to speak and act, to share our experience with others."

Batchelor (2015: 79) also sees a problem with the traditional notion of Nirvana as a specific supramundane experience, since this interpretation makes it "accessible only to trained meditators, thus conflicting with the account of it as 'immediate, clearly visible, inviting, uplifting, and personally sensed by the wise.'"

The reference to being immediate, etc., does not support the interpretation proposed. The immediacy mentioned here refers to the repercussions of the experience of Nirvana in removing defilements from the mind (translated by Bodhi 2012: 253). It is in this sense that Nirvana is indeed "clearly visible to ordinary people and accessible to them as a perspective from which they can live their everyday lives," to employ a formulation used by Batchelor (2015: 79). In other words, it is the very removal of defilements on attaining awakening that brings Nirvana right into the here and now of human experience. Hence, there is no need for Batchelor (2017: 24) to endeavor for Nirvana to "be restored to its rightful place at the heart of what it means each moment to be fully human." This rightful place has never been lost except by misunderstanding.

8. Rebirth

A Buddhist doctrine that has been of little appeal in secular circles is rebirth. Yet, early Buddhist descriptions of how to progress to the realization of Nirvana take for granted the idea of rebirth. Stream entry as the first stage of awakening implies that one will not be reborn more than seven times at most, and with full awakening the prospect of future rebirth has been completely transcended (Anālayo 2018d: 34).

A survey of relevant passages in the early discourses shows the doctrine of rebirth to be a central element in the teachings of early Buddhism (Anālayo 2018d: 5–35). It does not necessarily follow, however, that practicing within a Buddhist framework requires blind adherence to this idea. The situation can be explored by distinguishing definitions of right view, the adopting of which is a requirement for embarking on the early Buddhist path of practice (Anālayo 2018d: 29–31).

The flat denial of the possibility of rebirth would count as an instance of wrong view and therefore is better avoided. In fact, at the current stage of our knowledge there is no incontrovertible evidence that either proves or disproves rebirth. Although the notion that the mind equals the brain is a paradigmatic assumption in much of modern science, to date this has never been conclusively proven.

Right view can take two forms. One of these involves an affirmation of rebirth, the other finds expression in the four noble truths. Someone uncomfortable with the idea of a continuation beyond death need not feel forced to accept rebirth as a matter of mere belief but could simply consider it an element of Buddhist thought presently beyond personal verification. As a guiding principle for actual practice, the four noble truths could be relied on.

Although the above considerations suggest that there is no need to *believe* in rebirth in order to be a practicing Buddhist, for those who wish to understand early Buddhist thought, there is definitely a need to try to *understand* the doctrine of rebirth. This holds in particular for those who wish to teach the Dharma to others. Given the centrality of rebirth, it is not possible to gain a proper understanding of early Buddhism without having at least a basic grasp of what this particular doctrine involves.

An understanding of the early Buddhist teachings related to rebirth requires in particular a comprehension of its relation to the doctrine of not self. As mentioned at the outset of this chapter, a supposed contrast between not self and rebirth was one of the strategies employed by

Christian missionaries. The same position continues to be advocated by a range of Secular Buddhists. A case in point is when Batchelor (1997: 36) reasons that "a central Buddhist idea, however, is that no such intrinsic self can be found ... how do we square this with rebirth?" In support of the impression of some inner inconsistency, Batchelor (2015: 300 and 3) refers to

> one of the metaphysical questions that Gotama refused to address. He said that knowing whether the animating spirit (*jīva*) and bodily matter (*sarira*) are identical or different would not be an aid in practicing the fourfold task. Buddhist proponents of rebirth tend to ignore this oft-repeated injunction and opt for a body-mind dualism. ...
>
> Although the Buddha may have presented his ideas in the context of multiple lifetimes, this oft-repeated passage implies that he did so for cultural and pragmatic reasons alone. ... To have affirmed the view that the mind is different from the body and will be reborn after death in another body would have made him no different from those wanderers and ascetics he declared to be blind.

The set of metaphysical questions, which the Buddha refused to take up, involves sets of alternatives, where one has to accept one of two opposing positions. To take up one or the other position is problematic, since from an early Buddhist perspective both involve presuppositions that are mistaken (Anālayo 2018d: 39–44). This is somewhat like asking a lifetime teetotaler if she has finally stopped drinking alcohol. If she replies in the affirmative, this implies that she has been drinking up to then, which is wrong. If she denies, this conveys the impression that she is still drinking, which is also mistaken.

One of these metaphysical questions, mentioned in the quote above, concerns whether the soul (*jīva*) is identical or different from the body. Once the existence of a soul is considered a fiction, it becomes impossible to either affirm or else deny such identity. This does not stand in contrast with the notion that continuity beyond life is possible for a process that does not involve such a soul.

Such continuity involves a reciprocal conditioning between consciousness on the one side and name-and-form on the other (Anālayo 2018d: 9–17). This teaching posits an interrelation between two processes, both of which involve aspects of the mind. On the one side stands consciousness as a changing process and on the other side stand those mental factors required for processing what one is conscious of ("name") together with the material dimension of subjective experience ("form"). Quite definitely not involving a body-mind duality, the early Buddhist notion of rebirth does not stand in contrast to the doctrine of not self.

Although the doctrine of rebirth need not be accepted on faith alone as an authoritarian truth claim by a religious institution, it does call for a sincere attempt to understand its main parameters in order to be sufficiently equipped to interpret early Buddhist teachings on their own terms (Anālayo 2019i).

9. The Four Noble Truths

According to tradition, the four noble truths are the first teaching given by the Buddha. Figure 12 portrays the delivery of this first teaching, which set in motion the wheel of Dharma.

The four noble truths describe an awakening experience of the Buddha after having recollected his own past lives and directly witnessed the passing away and being reborn of others. The formulation of these truths clearly presupposes the doctrine of rebirth and needs to be approached keeping this in mind.

In addition to reflecting the doctrine of rebirth, the teaching on the four truths appears to be modeled on an ancient Indian scheme of medical diagnosis (Anālayo 2015d: 27–40). Batchelor (2017: 96) believes this to be a later "commentarial device with authoritarian undertones, introduced to justify the incongruous ordering" of the four truths. This assessment is not correct. The correlation with medical diagnosis is already found in

Figure 12. The Buddha Sets in Motion the Wheel of Dharma
by Teaching the Four Noble Truths; Sārnāth.

early discourses reflecting two distinct transmission lineages. It has for
this reason a claim to be representative of early Buddhist thought, even
though neither of these two transmission lineages are reflected in the Pāli
discourses. Here it needs to be kept in mind that the role of Pāli as the sole
authority for deciding what is early does not reflect our current academic
knowledge (see p. 78).

Without carrying authoritarian undertones, the medical scheme of diagnosis provides a meaningful perspective on the Buddha's adoption of the

scheme of four truths when he began to teach. In a philosophical setting brimming with various views and opinions, it makes sense to choose a medical precedent in order to convey a novel and pragmatic approach, thereby expressing what has been realized in ways already familiar to the audience.

The first truth diagnoses the condition of *dukkha*; the etiology of the second truth involves the identification of craving as a chief condition for *dukkha*; the prognosis in the third truth states that it is possible to become completely free from craving; and the treatment plan as the fourth truth takes the form of combining eight dimensions of practice into a path that interrelates ethical conduct with meditative cultivation of the mind and the growth of wisdom.

The standard formulation of the first truth lists old age, disease, and death in its diagnosis of *dukkha*. Yet Batchelor (2015: 70) considers the gist of this teaching to be an encouragement to "embrace life." Batchelor (2017: 104) then reasons that

> to fully embrace suffering does not increase suffering but paradoxically enhances your sense of astonishment at being alive. By saying "yes" to birth, sickness, aging, and death, you open your heart and mind to the sheer mystery of being here at all.

An interpretation of the first truth as being an encouragement to embrace life stands in direct contrast to the significance of old age, disease, and death as what motivated the future Buddha to go forth in quest of awakening (translated by Ñāṇamoli 1995/2005: 256). The parallel versions of this discourse agree in considering it ignoble to pursue what is subject to these three predicaments (translated by Anālayo 2012b: 23). Instead, one should seek what leads beyond these. Although such a quest is based on the cultivation of mindfulness as a way of coming fully alive to the present moment, its orientation is the opposite of embracing life as a value in and of itself.

Needless to say, anyone is of course free to adopt the idea of embracing life as a personal philosophy of life. The issue is only that such a celebration of the mystery of being alive does not correspond to the implications of the four truths in early Buddhist thought and hence cannot be considered an accurate reflection of this core element of the teachings.

The second truth identifies craving as a central condition for *dukkha*. Batchelor (2017: 89), however, reasons that the relationship between these two should be the opposite, in that *dukkha* should be considered the condition for craving. This is presumably meant to correct what Stephen Batchelor perceives as an "incongruous ordering" of the four truths, since on adopting his suggestion the cause comes first and the result afterward.

The reversal of sequence obtained by positing *dukkha* as what leads to craving, whatever its subjective appeal, is not an accurate reflection of early Buddhist thought (Anālayo 2013a: 30n60 and 2019a). Given the medical precedent for the four truths, it is only to be expected that the first truth mentions the effect and the second its cause. Instead of requiring correction by inverting their conditional relationship, it simply needs to be taken into account that the formulation of the four noble truths is not a statement of causality in the style of a flowchart, where the cause should invariably come before the result. In a medical scheme of diagnosis, a recognition of the symptoms comes before searching for the pathogen responsible for them. Without proper identification of the actual condition of the disease, how could one set out to search for the virus that has caused it? For this reason, *dukkha* should indeed be mentioned first and craving only subsequently.

Although craving can occur when confronted with pain, it can similarly manifest in reaction to what is pleasant or even neutral. Hence, it would not do to assume that craving is caused only by manifestations of *dukkha*, such as old age, disease, and death mentioned above. Moreover, the only early discourse that takes conditioned arising beyond *dukkha*, in an exposition sometimes referred to as "transcendental dependent arising," mentions a whole series of conditions that can result from *dukkha*, none of which is craving (translated by Bodhi 2000: 555).

The present instance reflects the importance of taking into account the doctrine of rebirth. Early Buddhist thought considers the existential *dukkha* that pervades ordinary human life since conception to be the result of craving that has been present prior to conception. In fact, according to early Buddhist thought craving serves to support the transition from one life to another (translated Bodhi 2000: 1393). This is comparable to the transition of fire, such as from one tree to another in a forest fire, which has wind as its support.

By ignoring the rebirth background, it becomes difficult to assess the relationship between craving and *dukkha* adequately, to understand why craving is qualified as leading to renewed existence, and why the destruction of craving equals the transcendence of future rebirth. To repeat the point already made above, understanding the doctrine of the four noble truths does not require belief in former lives. But it does require taking into account the notion of former lives in order to gain a proper understanding of the teaching conveyed by the four noble truths.

In line with his reversal of the relationship between the first and the second truths, Batchelor (2017: 100) also inverts the other two truths, proposing that the eightfold path should be considered the goal. This proposal overlooks a distinction made in the early discourses between the eightfold path as the means to reach awakening and the continuity of these same qualities and practices, once the final goal has been reached, as a tenfold path (e.g. translated by Ñāṇamoli 1995/2005: 550 and 939). With full awakening attained, each of the factors of the eightfold path undergoes a change from having been the path factor of a trainee to becoming the path factor of one beyond training. In addition to such upgrading of the eight factors, a fully awakened one is endowed with two extra path factors, namely right knowledge and right liberation. Thus, the eightfold path is not the final goal itself but the means leading to the final goal.

10. The Notion of Truth

The notion of truth as such is another topic that tends to be perceived as problematic in Secular Buddhist circles. Regarding the early Buddhist notion of truth, Batchelor (2017: 83–84) refers to a study of the Buddha's first discourse by Norman (1984), who shows how the expression 'noble truth' was inexpertly interpolated into the text at a later date than its original composition. But since no such original text has come down to us, we cannot know what it *did* say. All that can reasonably be deduced is that instead of talking of four noble truths, the text spoke merely of 'four.' The term 'noble truth' is so much taken for granted that we fail to notice its polemical, sectarian, and superior tone . . . one implication of Norman's discovery is that the Buddha may not have been concerned with the question of 'truth' at all. His awakening may have had little to do with gaining a veridical cognition of 'reality,' a privileged understanding that corresponds to the way things actually *are*.

In sum, according to Batchelor (2017: 86), "if Mr. Norman is correct, the Buddha may not have presented his ideas in terms of 'truth' at all." A perusal of the relevant article by K. R. Norman brings to light that the idea is only that an addition of the expression "noble truth" in the first discourse would have been inspired by occurrences of this expression in short statements found elsewhere in the Pāli texts. The relevant part in Norman (1984: 387), which is based on designating different occurrences of the expression noble truth (*ariya-sacca*) as "enlightenment," "gerundival," and "mnemonic" sets, proceeds as follows:

> The word *ariya-sacca* is not appropriate in the 'enlightenment' (§5.1) or the 'gerundival' (§4.3) sets, but its presence in the 'mnemonic' set doubtless led to its introduction there by analogy.

The proposal implies that the occurrence of the expression "noble truth" in some statements would have led to the same expression being used also in other passages, where it was not originally found. This does not imply that early Buddhist thought did not have a notion of truth as such. Stephen Batchelor's conclusions derive from a misunderstanding of K. R. Norman's research.

11. SUBJECTIVE BELIEF

In recognition of the influence of Stephen Batchelor's writings on many Secular Buddhists, in what follows I briefly explore what might explain the genesis of some of his ways of presenting early Buddhist teachings (and related academic research). In relation to the Buddhist doctrine of rebirth, for example, Batchelor (2011: 38–39) reports:

> I rebelled against the very idea of [a] body-mind dualism. I could not accept that my experience was ontologically divided into two incommensurable spheres: one material, the other mental. Rationally, I found the idea incoherent. Yet this is what I was being asked (told) to believe.

The passage points to the centrality of the assumption that the Buddhist doctrine of rebirth involves a mind-body dualism. The resultant experience of dissonance would presumably have motivated a reinterpretation of various teachings, such as the four truths, in a way that does away with their intrinsic relationship to the notion of rebirth. Yet, the assumption itself is simply mistaken, as the Buddhist doctrine of rebirth does not involve a mind-body dualism. Instead of requiring a major reinterpretation of the teachings, a better understanding of them could have solved the dilemma.

Another relevant passage is a report by Batchelor (1990: 10) of a mystical experience he had in India while carrying a water bucket through a forest on the way back to his hut:

> I was then suddenly brought to a halt by the upsurge of an overwhelming sense of the sheer mystery of everything. It was as though I were lifted up onto the crest of a shivering wave which abruptly swelled from the ocean that was life itself. How is it that people can be unaware of this most obvious question? I asked myself. How can anyone pass their life without responding to it? This experience lasted in its full intensity for only a few minutes. It was not an illumination in which some final,

mystical truth became momentarily very clear. For it gave me no answers. It only revealed the massiveness of the question. From that time on my practice of Buddhism has been one of unravelling the perception of life and the world revealed in those moments.

According to detailed research on meditation-related experiences by Vieten et al. (2018: 12), mystical experiences are more common than ordinarily assumed, as "in the general public, 30–50% of people report having had what they would consider a mystical experience." Characteristic of those who have such experiences can often be "an intuitive belief that the experience is a source of objective truth about the nature of reality." In the present case, Stephen Batchelor in fact explicitly indicates that "unravelling the perception of life and the world revealed" to him in his mystical experience has been the guiding principle in his involvement with Buddhism. In particular the inconclusive nature of the experience in question appears to have influenced Stephen Batchelor's ideas about the nature of Nirvana and awakening, discussed above, viewed by him as if these were accurate reflections of early Buddhist thought.

The rebellious reaction against an assumed body-mind dualism and the apparent tendency to read early Buddhist accounts of awakening in the light of a personal experience point to an inability to separate what the texts say from how one interprets them, resulting in a projection onto the original of one's subjective views. The need for authentication of this projection in turn seems to rely on strategies adopted in various Buddhist traditions of pretending that their particular ideas go back to the historical Buddha.

All of this converges in turn on the conceit of being superior to other Buddhist traditions. This becomes patently evident when Batchelor (2017: 80) envisions his own contribution as involving the construction of "Buddhism 2.0," implying all the diverse forms of Buddhism in existence are only Buddhism 1.0. The contrast made here relies on a standard way of referring to a revised version of a computer program as "2.0." The idea of updating Buddhism from 1.0 to 2.0 has its complement in a dismissive attitude toward existing Buddhist traditions, representative of the outdated "Buddhism 1.0." This can be seen in the following evaluation by Batchelor (2015: 313–14):

> From a modern perspective, many of the traditional forms of Buddhism inherited from Asia appear to be stagnating. They seem primarily intent on preserving time-honored doctrines and practices by endlessly repeating past teachings and instructions ... A contemporary culture of awakening is unlikely to emerge from the traditional schools of Buddhism without outside impetus. For a stagnant culture to flower will require a return to the often ignored or forgotten sources of the tradition, a systematic unlearning of outdated Buddhist dogma, a radical transformation of institutions, and a concerted effort to rethink the dharma from the ground up.

Based on considering Asian Buddhists as following antiquated forms of Buddhism in need of renewal, Stephen Batchelor's writings inadvertently continue on the track set by Christian missionaries. They do so by rejecting the Buddha's claim to have reached awakening, discarding the transformative nature of Nirvana, alleging that the rebirth doctrine is incoherent, and dismissing the three refuges. A chief difference seems to be that, instead of serving as a means to convert Buddhists to Christianity, the thrust is rather to inculcate a materialistic worldview.

12. METHODOLOGY

Needless to say, Secular Buddhists in general and Stephen Batchelor in particular are of course free to have their own opinions in whatever way they wish. If for them Nirvana is merely a temporary moment of relief and defilements cannot be eradicated, so be it. The discussion in the present chapter is not about censoring anyone's personal beliefs and ideas, nor is it in defense of a religious institution or composed out of allegiance to its authority. However, Stephen Batchelor presents certain claims about early Buddhism. As an integral part of the scientific procedure of knowledge production, scholars critically evaluate hypotheses and conclusions presented by others.

From this viewpoint, it is revealing to take a look at how Batchelor (2010/2011: 101) explains the methodology he adopted in order to develop his understanding of Buddhism. He read through the Pāli discourses in their English translations in the following way:

> anything attributed to him [i.e. the Buddha] that could just as well have been said in the classical Indian texts of the Upanishads or Vedas, I would bracket off and put to one side. Having done this, I would then have to see whether what I had sifted out as the Buddha's word provided an adequate foundation for formulating a coherent vision for leading a contemporary lay Buddhist life.

From a methodological perspective, this approach makes personal assumptions the guiding principle for data selection, rather than testing such assumptions against the whole body of data available. Take for example the proposed reading of descriptions of awakening and Nirvana, seemingly done in the light of the limitations of a personal mystical experience. This ignores all relevant early Buddhist texts, and those relevant to this topic are certainly not material to be bracketed off as something that could as well have been said in other classical Indian texts.

Another aspect related to methodology emerges in relation to presenting the research by Norman (1984) as implying that the Buddha did not formulate his ideas in terms of truth at all. After this reasoning had appeared in print (Batchelor 2012: 92–93), I replied (Anālayo 2013a: 16), correcting this misunderstanding of Norman's research. Before publication, I had shown a draft version of the article to Stephen Batchelor and the published article acknowledges his feedback.

Nevertheless, four years later Batchelor (2017: 83–86) republished the same claim without adjusting it or referring to the criticism that had been voiced, of which he obviously was aware. The issue at stake is not just a matter of different viewpoints; his interpretation of the research by K. R. Norman is simply wrong. Admittedly, the article by K. R. Norman is cryptic and not easy to follow, but once it has been clarified that a misunderstanding has occurred, it is not appropriate to continue repeating it without at least acknowledging the existence of criticism in order to provide readers with the possibility to follow up and come to their own conclusions. Such lack of properly informing his readers reflects a danger inherent in the excessive desire to do away with the concept of truth; it can result in a loss of truthfulness.

A disinclination to meet basic scholarly standards is also evident from how Stephen Batchelor defends his translations, which at times no longer reflect the original. Batchelor (2017: 9 and 19–20) affirms that "my priorities are not the same as those of a scholar," followed by reasoning that

> If one's primary relation to the text is that of a detached philologist, then one's concern will be to judge the literal accuracy of the translation; but if it is that of a practitioner engaged in an existential dialogue with Gotama, then one will seek a reading that helps one flourish as a person ... A dialogical relation with tradition, therefore, transforms not only the reader but also the texts that are being read. I also consider myself an artist. From an aesthetic perspective, I try to hear how these scriptures sing.... Over time, those passages that resonate for me at the same key and pitch have coalesced into the body of primary sources on which I build my understanding of what Gotama teaches.

The correctness of the translation of the text relied on for actual practice is crucial. This is not something of concern only to detached philologists. It is of course open to anyone to develop an existential dialogue with the texts for personal edification. But to use that as an excuse for publishing inaccurate translations is irresponsible and contrary to the basics of scholarly procedure.

In sum, due to intentionally making bias the main methodology for reading texts, ignoring published criticism of obvious misinterpretations, and advocating that correct translation does not matter, it seems that Stephen Batchelor should be taken at his word: he should not be considered a scholar. His writings could then perhaps be seen as a remarkable illustration of Western superiority conceit.

SUMMARY

The construction of the concept of "Buddhism" appears to have taken place on Asian soil at an early time, rather than being a nineteenth-century idea invented in the West. Already the early discourses reflect the sense of some degree of institutional Buddhist identity, sufficient for it to be considered an -ism. The monastic Saṅgha as the third refuge of a Buddhist is an early element, as is the notion that the Buddha, as the first refuge, had eradicated all defilements when realizing Nirvana on the night of his awakening. The attainment of levels of awakening does not imply a transcendence of a concern with adhering to rules of moral conduct.

Although the doctrine of rebirth need not be accepted on blind faith, its implications need to be understood in order to be able to make sense of the early Buddhist teachings. This holds even for the key teaching of the four noble truths. The sequence of presentation of the four truths appears to reflect an ancient Indian model of medical diagnosis and hence is not in need of reordering. Moreover, current academic research on the formulation of the Buddha's first teaching does not imply that the notion of truth as such is a later element.

Stephen Batchelor's secular "Buddhism without beliefs" turns out to be rather his secular beliefs without Buddhism. Instead of being an innocent questioning of outdated religious dogmas, his writings inadvertently continue Christian missionary strategies originally developed to undermine Buddhism.

The appeal of this approach among those unaware of the misunderstandings involved appears to be in part related to a resonance with an iconoclastic attitude. Such an attitude is a natural result of the experience of cognitive dissonance from the encounter between two different cultures, in the present case the Western worldview encountering certain Asian Buddhist teachings. The resultant rebelliousness against anything perceived as "religious" on the side of those influenced by Western materialist values combines with the relative newness of Buddhism in the West and hence the comparatively short period of exposure to its ideas. Yet, perhaps by now the time has come for Western Buddhists to enter into a more mature relationship with the teachings and with other Buddhist traditions, letting go of superiority conceit and finding a middle path aloof from the two extremes of blind acceptance and equally blind rejection.

Conclusions

The material presented in the four chapters of this book is meant to highlight the need to recognize superiority conceit in its androcentric, Mahāyāna, Theravāda, and Secular Buddhist manifestations. It is simply a form of bondage for men to look down on women as not fit to take monastic leadership roles or be advanced bodhisattvas, for those who intend to become future Buddhas to look down on those not aspiring for Buddhahood as inferior, for Theravādins to look down on others as deviant from the original true teaching, or for Secular Buddhists to look down on traditional Buddhists as stagnant dogmatists caught up in rituals who lack a proper understanding of the teachings of the historical Buddha.

Following the Buddha's example and putting his vision into practice requires stepping out of all of these forms of superiority conceit. Women must be accorded the full right to embark on the monastic life and to be recognized as advanced bodhisattvas. The derogatory attitude implicit in "Hināyāna" rhetoric is not compatible with genuine compassion and to some extent even runs counter to progress to Buddhahood, which after all is about giving up conceit. The claim by followers of the Pāli tradition to be the sole true heirs of the Buddha is also not conducive to growth in the qualities required for awakening. Western Buddhism is just another branch growing from the bodhi tree, neither intrinsically better nor intrinsically worse than Asian Buddhist traditions.

Instead of appropriating the historical Buddha to authenticate one's personal or group beliefs, the true seal of authentication for any Buddhist practitioner can be found by putting into practice the central discovery of the historical Buddha: emptiness, or not self. It is by diminishing ego, letting go of arrogance, and abandoning conceit that one becomes a better Buddhist, no matter what tradition one may follow.

The need to give up superiority conceit in its various Buddhist manifestations is required not only from the viewpoint of Buddhist doctrine, but also in light of the current crisis faced by humanity on this planet. The superiority conceit of human beings in relation to the natural environment, in the form of the assumption that nature can be exploited without concern for possible consequences, has led to a crisis: the repercussions of climate change and ecological destruction are threatening to escalate to a point at which human life on this planet can no longer be sustained. It is already too late to prevent a mass extinction of species and a serious deterioration of living conditions. But it is not yet too late to prevent a total catastrophe.

In this situation, members of all Buddhist traditions need to collaborate in a spirit of mutual respect, in order to apply the medicine of the Dharma for maximum effect in countering the mental disease responsible for the current crisis. The historical Buddha's teachings on ethics of the mind can be relied on to counter the irresponsibility of materialism and its rampant greed, together with employing the practices of Buddhist mental culture to find a middle path between the extremes of denial and despair (Anālayo 2019g and 2019k). In this way, as an expression of the conjunction of compassion and emptiness as well as an implementation of internal and external dimensions of mindfulness, stepping out of various forms of superiority conceit could pave the way for a collaboration of members of all Buddhist traditions in doing the needful to ensure that future generations can still benefit from the liberating message of the Buddha.

Bibliography

Anālayo. 2003. *Satipaṭṭhāna: The Direct Path to Realization*. Birmingham: Windhorse Publications. https://www.buddhismuskunde.uni-hamburg.de/ pdf/5-personen/analayo/direct-path.pdf

———. 2005. "The Seven Stages of Purification in Comparative Perspective." *Journal of Buddhist Studies* 3: 126–38. https://www.buddhismuskunde.uni-hamburg.de/pdf/5-personen/analayo/seven-stages-purif.pdf

———. 2009a. "The Treaties on the Path to Liberation (解脫道論) and the Visuddhimagga." *Fuyan Buddhist Studies* 4: 1–15. https://www.buddhismuskunde. uni-hamburg.de/pdf/5-personen/analayo/treatise-path-liberation.pdf

———. 2009b. "Yodhājīva Sutta." In *Encyclopaedia of Buddhism, Volume 8*, edited by W.G. Weeraratne, 798–99. Sri Lanka: Department of Buddhist Affairs. https://www.buddhismuskunde.uni-hamburg.de/pdf/5-personen/analayo/ encyclopedia-entries/yodhajiva.pdf

———. 2010a. *From Grasping to Emptiness—Excursions into the Thought-World of the Pāli Discourses (2)*. New York: Buddhist Association of the United States. https://www.buddhismuskunde.uni-hamburg.de/pdf/5-personen/analayo/ from-grasping.pdf

———. 2010b. *The Genesis of the Bodhisattva Ideal*. Hamburg: Hamburg University Press. https://www.buddhismuskunde.uni-hamburg.de/pdf/5-personen/ analayo/genesis-bodhisattva.pdf

———. 2011. *A Comparative Study of the Majjhima-nikāya*. Taipei: Dharma Drum Publishing Corporation. https://www.buddhismuskunde.uni-hamburg.de /pdf/5-personen/analayo/compstudyvol1.pdf; https://www.buddhismus kunde.uni-hamburg.de/pdf/5-personen/analayo/compstudyvol2.pdf

———. 2012a. "The Dynamics of Theravāda Insight Meditation." In 佛教禪坐傳統國際學術研討 會論文集 [*Buddhist Meditation Traditions: An*

International Symposium], edited by Kuo-pin Chuang, 23–56. Taiwan: Dharma Drum Publishing Corporation. https://www.buddhismuskunde. uni-hamburg.de/pdf/5-personen/analayo/dynamicsinsight.pdf

——— 2012b. *Madhyama-āgama Studies.* Taipei: Dharma Drum Publishing Corporation. https://www.buddhismuskunde.uni-hamburg.de/pdf/ 5-personen/analayo/mastudies.pdf

——— 2012c. "Purification in Early Buddhist Discourse and Buddhist Ethics." *Bukkyō Kenkyū* 40: 67–97. https://www.buddhismuskunde.uni-hamburg. de/pdf/5-personen/analayo/purification-in-early-buddhist-discourse.pdf

——— 2013a. "The Chinese Parallels to the Dhammacakkappavattana-sutta (2)." *Journal of the Oxford Centre for Buddhist Studies* 5: 9–41. https://www.buddhismuskunde.uni-hamburg.de/pdf/5-personen/analayo/ dhammacakka2.pdf

——— 2013b. *Perspectives on Satipaṭṭhāna.* Cambridge: Windhorse Publications. https://www.buddhismuskunde.uni-hamburg.de/pdf/5-personen/analayo/ perspectives.pdf

——— 2014a. "On the Bhikkhunī Ordination Controversy." *Sri Lanka International Journal of Buddhist Studies* 3: 1–20. https://www.buddhismuskunde. uni-hamburg.de/pdf/5-personen/analayo/bhikkhuni-controversy.pdf

——— 2014b. *The Dawn of Abhidharma.* Hamburg: Hamburg University Press. https://www.buddhismuskunde.uni-hamburg.de/pdf/5-personen/analayo/ dawn-abhidharma.pdf

——— 2015a. *Compassion and Emptiness in Early Buddhist Meditation.* Cambridge: Windhorse Publications. https://www.buddhismuskunde.uni-hamburg.de/pdf/5-personen/analayo/compassionemptiness.pdf

——— 2015b. "Compassion in the Āgamas and Nikāyas." *Dharma Drum Journal of Buddhist Studies* 16: 1–30. https://www.buddhismuskunde.uni-hamburg. de/pdf/5-personen/analayo/compassion.pdf

——— 2015c. "The Cullavagga on Bhikkhunī Ordination." *Journal of Buddhist Ethics* 22: 401–48. https://www.buddhismuskunde.uni-hamburg.de/ pdf/5-personen/analayo/cullavagga.pdf

——— 2015d. *Saṃyukta-āgama Studies.* Taipei: Dharma Drum Publishing Corporation. https://www.buddhismuskunde.uni-hamburg.de/pdf/5-personen/ analayo/sastudies.pdf

—— 2016a. *Ekottarika-āgama Studies*. Taipei: Dharma Drum Publishing Corporation. https://www.buddhismuskunde.uni-hamburg.de/pdf/ 5-personen/analayo/ekottarikastudies.pdf

—— 2016b. *The Foundation History of the Nuns' Order*. Bochum: Projektverlag. https://www.buddhismuskunde.uni-hamburg.de/pdf/5-personen/analayo/ foundation.pdf

—— 2016c. *Mindfully Facing Disease and Death: Compassionate Advice from Early Buddhist Texts*. Cambridge: Windhorse Publications. https://www. buddhismuskunde.uni-hamburg.de/pdf/5-personen/analayo/climate.pdf

—— 2017a. *Buddhapada and the Bodhisattva Path*. Bochum: Projektverlag. https://www.buddhismuskunde.uni-hamburg.de/pdf/5-personen/analayo/ buddhapada.pdf

—— 2017b. *Dīrgha-āgama Studies*. Taipei: Dharma Drum Publishing Corporation. https://www.buddhismuskunde.uni-hamburg.de/pdf/5-personen/ analayo/dastudies.pdf

—— 2017c. *Early Buddhist Meditation Studies*. Barre: Barre Center for Buddhist Studies. https://www.buddhismuskunde.uni-hamburg.de/pdf/ 5-personen/analayo/ebms.pdf

—— 2017d. "How Compassion Became Painful." *Journal of Buddhist Studies* 14: 85–113. https://www.buddhismuskunde.uni-hamburg.de/pdf/5-personen/ analayo/compassionpainful.pdf

—— 2017e. "The Luminous Mind in Theravāda and Dharmaguptaka Discourses." *Journal of the Oxford Centre for Buddhist Studies* 13: 10–51. https://www.buddhismuskunde.uni-hamburg.de/pdf/5-personen/analayo/ luminousmind.pdf

—— 2017f. *A Meditator's Life of the Buddha: Based on the Early Discourses*. Cambridge: Windhorse Publications.

—— 2017g. "Theravāda Vinaya and Bhikkhunī Ordination." In *Rules of Engagement: Medieval Traditions of Buddhist Monastic Regulations*, edited by S. Andrews, J. Chen, and C. Liu, 333–67. Bochum: Projekt Verlag. https://www.buddhismuskunde.uni-hamburg.de/pdf/5-personen/analayo/ theravadavinaya.pdf

—— 2017h. "The Validity of Bhikkhunī Ordination by Bhikkhus Only, According to the Pāli Vinaya," *Journal of the Oxford Centre for Buddhist Studies*

12: 9–25. https://www.buddhismuskunde.uni-hamburg.de/pdf/5-personen/analayo/validity.pdf

———— 2017i. *Vinaya Studies*. Taipei: Dharma Drum Publishing Corporation. https://www.buddhismuskunde.uni-hamburg.de/pdf/5-personen/analayo/vinayastudies.pdf

———— 2018a. *Bhikkhunī Ordination from Ancient India to Contemporary Sri Lanka*. New Taipei City: Āgama Research Group. https://www.buddhism uskunde.uni-hamburg.de/pdf/5-personen/analayo/bhikkhuni.pdf

———— 2018b. "Bhikṣuṇī Ordination." In *Oxford Handbook of Buddhist Ethics*, edited by D. Cozort and J.M. Shields, 116–34. Oxford: Oxford University Press.

———— 2018c. "The Case for Reviving the Bhikkhunī Order by Single Ordination." *Journal of Buddhist Ethics* 25: 931–62. https://www.buddhismuskunde. uni-hamburg.de/pdf/5-personen/analayo/case.pdf

———— 2018d. *Rebirth in Early Buddhism and Contemporary Research*. Boston: Wisdom Publications.

———— 2019a. "Craving and *Dukkha*." *Insight Journal* 45: 35–42. https://www.bud dhismuskunde.uni-hamburg.de/pdf/5-personen/analayo/cravingdukkha.pdf

———— 2019b. "Definitions of Right Concentration in Comparative Perspective." *Singaporean Journal of Buddhist Studies*, 5: 9–39.

———— 2019c. "How Mindfulness Came to Plunge into Its Objects." *Mindfulness* 10.6: 1181–85.

———— 2019d. "Immeasurable Meditations and Mindfulness." *Mindfulness* 10.12: 2620–28.

———— 2019e. "The Insight Knowledge of Fear and Adverse Effects of Mindfulness Practices." *Mindfulness* 10.10: 2172–85.

———— 2019f. "Meditation on the Breath: Mindfulness and Focused Attention." *Mindfulness* 10.8: 1684–91.

———— 2019g. *Mindfully Facing Climate Change*, Barre: Barre Center for Buddhist Studies. https://www.buddhismuskunde.uni-hamburg.de/pdf/5-personen/analayo/climate.pdf

———— 2019h. *Mindfulness of Breathing: A Practice Guide and Translations*. Cambridge: Windhorse Publications.

———— 2019i. "Rebirth and the West." *Insight Journal* 45: 55–64.

—— 2019j. "The Role of Mindfulness in the Cultivation of Absorption." *Mindfulness* 10.11: 2341–51.

—— 2019k. "A Task for Mindfulness: Facing Climate Change." *Mindfulness* 10.9: 1926–35.

—— 2019l. "Women in Early Buddhism." *Journal of Buddhist Studies* 16: 33–76.

—— 2020a. "A Brief History of Buddhist Absorption." *Mindfulness* 11.3: 571–586.

—— 2020b. "Confronting Racism with Mindfulness." *Mindfulness* 11: 2283–2297.

—— 2020c. "Dependent Arising." *Insight Journal* 46: 1–8.

—— 2020d. 'Mūlasarvāstivādin and Sarvāstivādin': Oral Transmission Lineages of Āgama Texts." In *Research on the Saṃyukta-āgama*, edited by Bhikkhunī Dhammadinnā, 387–426. Taipei: Dharma Drum Publishing Corporation.

—— 2020e. "The Tevijjavacchagotta-sutta and the Anupada-sutta in Relation to the Emergence of Abhidharma Thought." *Journal of Buddhist Studies* 17 (forthcoming).

Arbel, Keren. 2017. *Early Buddhist Meditation: The Four Jhānas as the Actualization of Insight*. Oxon: Routledge.

Attwood, Jayarava. 2018. "The Buddhas of the Three Times and the Chinese Origins of the Heart Sutra." *Journal of the Oxford Centre for Buddhist Studies* 15: 9–27.

Batchelor, Stephen. 1983. *Alone with Others: An Existential Approach to Buddhism.* New York: Grove Weidenfeld.

—— 1990. *The Faith to Doubt: Glimpses of Buddhist Uncertainty.* Berkeley: Parallax Press.

—— 1994. *The Awakening of the West: The Encounter of Buddhism and Western Culture.* Berkeley: Parallax Press.

—— 1997. *Buddhism Without Beliefs: A Contemporary Guide to Awakening.* New York: Riverhead Books.

—— 2010/2011. *Confession of a Buddhist Atheist.* New York: Spiegel & Grau Trade Paperbacks.

—— 2012: "A Secular Buddhism." *Journal of Global Buddhism* 13: 87–107.

—— 2014. *Living with the Devil: A Meditation on Good and Evil.* New York: Riverhead Books.

———— 2015. *After Buddhism: Rethinking the Dharma for a Secular Age*. New Haven: Yale University Press.

———— 2017. *Secular Buddhism: Imagining the Dharma in an Uncertain World*. New Haven: Yale University Press.

Benn, James A. 2007. *Burning for the Buddha: Self-Immolation in Chinese Buddhism*. Honolulu: University of Hawai'i Press.

Blum, Mark L. 2013. *The Nirvana Sutra (Mahāparinirvāṇa-sūtra) Volume I (Taishō Volume 12, Number 374), Translated from the Chinese*. Berkeley: Bukkyo Dendo Kyokai America.

Bodhi, Bhikkhu. 2000. *The Connected Discourses of the Buddha: A New Translation of the Saṃyutta Nikāya*. Somerville: Wisdom Publications.

———— 2012. *The Numerical Discourses of the Buddha: A Translation of the Aṅguttara Nikāya*. Somerville: Wisdom Publications.

———— 2017. *The Suttanipāta: An Ancient Collection of Buddha's Discourses, Together with Its Commentaries—Paramatthajotikā II and Excerpts from the Niddesa*. Boston: Wisdom Publications.

Bretfeld, Sven. 2012. "Resonant Paradigms in the Study of Religions and the Emergence of Theravāda Buddhism." *Religion* 42.2: 273–97.

Braun, Erik. 2013. *The Birth of Insight: Meditation, Modern Buddhism, and the Burmese Monk Ledi Sayadaw*. Chicago: University of Chicago Press.

Carter, John R. 1993. "The Origin and Development of 'Buddhism' and 'Religion' in the Study of the Theravāda Buddhist Tradition." In *On Understanding Buddhists: Essays on the Theravāda Tradition in Sri Lanka*, edited by John R. Carter, 9–25. Albany: State University of New York Press.

Chandawimala, Rangama. 2008. "Bodhisattva Practice in Sri Lankan Buddhism with Special Reference to the Abhayagiri Fraternity." *Indian International Journal of Buddhist Studies* 9: 23–43.

Chang Garma C. C. 1983. *A Treasury of Mahāyāna Sūtras: Selections from the Mahāratnakūṭa Sūtra*. University Park: The Pennsylvania State University Press.

Collett, Alice. 2018. "Buddhism and Women." In *Oxford Handbook of Buddhist Ethics*, edited by D. Cozort and J.M. Shields, 552–66. Oxford: Oxford University Press.

Collett, Alice, and Anālayo. 2014. "Bhikkhave and Bhikkhu as Gender-

Inclusive Terminology in Early Buddhist Texts." *Journal of Buddhist Ethics* 21: 760–97.

Collins, Steven. 1990. "Introduction." In *Buddhist Monastic Life: According to the Texts of the Theravāda Tradition*, M. Wijayaratne, ix–xxiv. Cambridge: Cambridge University Press.

—— 1998. *Nirvana and Other Buddhist Felicities: Utopias of the Pali Imaginaire*. Cambridge: University Press.

Davidson, Ronald M. 2002. *Indian Esoteric Buddhism: A Social History of the Tantric Movement*. New York: Colombia University Press.

Deokar, Mahesh A. 2012. "Understanding Māgadhī: The Pure Speech of the Buddha." *Journal of Buddhist Studies* 10: 119–35.

Dhammadinnā, Bhikkhunī. 2015. "Women's Predictions to Buddhahood in Middle-Period Literature." *Journal of Buddhist Ethics* 22: 481–531.

—— 2015/2016. "Women's Aspirations and Soteriological Agency in Sarvāstivāda and Mūlasarvāstivāda Vinaya Narratives." *Journal of Buddhism, Law & Society*, 1: 33–67.

—— 2018. "Karma Here and Now in a Mūlasarvāstivāda Avadāna: How the Bodhisattva Changed Sex and was Born as a Female 500 Times." *Annual Report of the International Research Institute for Advanced Buddhology at Soka University* 21: 63–94.

Endo Tochiichi. 1996. "Bodhisattas in the Pāli Commentaries." *Bukkyō Kenkyū* 25: 65–92.

—— 2004. "The Disappearance of the True Dhamma (Saddhamma-antaradhāna): Pāli Commentarial Interpretations." In *Encounters with the World: Essays to Honour Aloysius Pieris S.J. on His 70th Birthday 9th April 2004*, edited by R. Crusz, M. Fernando, and A. Tilakaratne, 235–55. Nugegoda: Ecumenical Institute for Study & Dialogue.

Freiberger, Oliver. 2000. *Der Orden in der Lehre: Zur religiösen Deutung des Saṅgha im frühen Buddhismus*. Wiesbaden: Harrassowitz.

Frauwallner, Erich. 1956. *The Earliest Vinaya and the Beginnings of Buddhist Literature*. Rome: Istituto Italiano per il Medio ed Estremo Oriente.

Geiger, Wilhelm. 1912. *The Mahāvaṃsa or The Great Chronicle of Ceylon, Translated into English*. London: Pali Text Society.

Gethin, Rupert. 1992. *The Buddhist Path to Awakening: A Study of the Bodhi-Pakkhiyā Dhammā*. Leiden: E.J. Brill.

—— 1994. "*Bhavaṅga* and Rebirth According to the Abhidhamma." In *The Buddhist Forum III*, edited by T. Skorupski and U. Pagel, 11–35. London: School of Oriental and African Studies, University of London.

—— 2016. "The Buddhist Faith of Non-Buddhists: From Dual Belonging to Dual Attachment." In *Buddhist Christian Dual Belonging: Affirmations, Objections, Explorations*, edited by G. D'Costa and R. Thompson, 179–95. Farnham: Ashgate.

Gombrich, Richard F. 1988. *Theravāda Buddhism: A Social History from Ancient Benares to Modern Colombo.* London: Routledge & Kegan Paul.

—— 2007. "Popperian Vinaya: Conjecture and Refutation in Practice." In *Pramāṇakīrtiḥ: Papers Dedicated to Ernst Steinkellner on the Occasion of His 70th Birthday*, edited by B. Kellner, H. Krasser, H. Lasic, M. T. Much, and H. Tauscher, 203–11. Wien: Arbeitskreis für Tibetische und Buddhistische Studien, Universität Wien.

Harris, Elizabeth J. 2006. *Theravāda Buddhism and the British Encounter: Religious, Missionary and Colonial Experience in Nineteenth Century Sri Lanka.* Oxon: Routledge.

Harrison, Paul. 1987. "Who Gets to Ride in the Great Vehicle? Self-Image and Identity Among the Followers of the Early Mahāyāna." *Journal of the International Association of Buddhist Studies* 10.1: 67–89.

—— 1995. "Some Reflections on the Personality of the Buddha." *Otani Gakuho* 74.4: 1–29.

Harvey, Peter. 2007. "Bodhisattva Career in the Theravāda." In *Encyclopedia of Buddhism*, edited by D. Keown and C.S. Prebish, 83–87. London: Routledge.

Heinsius, Daniel. 1616. *Clementis Alexandrini Opera Graece et Latine Quae Extant.* Leiden: Excudit Ioannes Patius Academiae Typographus Pro Bibliopolio Commeliniano.

Horner, I.B. 1938/1982: *The Book of the Discipline (Vinaya-Piṭaka), Volume IV (Mahāvagga).* London: Pali Text Society.

—— 1969. *Milinda's Questions, Volume I, Translated from the Pali.* London: Luzac & Company Ltd.

Ireland, John D. 1990. *The Udāna: Inspired Utterances of the Buddha.* Kandy: Buddhist Publication Society.

Jayawickrama, N.A. 1990. *The Story of Gotama Buddha: The Nidāna-kathā of the Jātakaṭṭhakathā.* Oxford: Pali Text Society.

Jurewicz, J. 2000. "Playing with Fire: The Pratītyasamutpāda from the Perspective of Vedic Thought." *Journal of the Pali Text Society* 26: 77–103.

Lamotte, Étienne. 1994. *The Teaching of Vimalakīrti (Vimalakīrinirdeśa): From the French Translation with Introduction and Notes (L'Enseignement de Vimalakīrti)*, translated by Sara Boin. Oxford: The Pali Text Society.

Law, Bimala Charan. 1923. *The Life and Work of Buddhaghosa*. Calcutta: Thacker, Spink & Co.

Lopez, Donald S. Jr. 1996. *Elaborations on Emptiness: Uses of the Heart Sūtra*. New Jersey: Princeton University Press.

Martini, Giuliana. 2013. "Bodhisattva Texts, Ideologies and Rituals in Khotan in the Fifth and Sixth Centuries." In *Buddhism Among the Iranian Peoples of Central Asia*, edited by M. De Chiara, M. Maggi, and G. Martini, 13–69. Vienna: Österreichische Akademie der Wissenschaften.

Nanjio Bunyiu. 1886. *A Short History of the Twelve Japanese Buddhist Sects: Translated from the Original Japanese*. Tokyo: Bukkyō-sho-ei-yaku-shuppan-sha.

Ñāṇamoli, Bhikkhu. 1991. *The Path of Purification (Visuddhimagga) by Bhadantācariya Buddhaghosa*. Kandy: Buddhist Publication Society.

———— 1995/2005. *The Middle Length Discourses of the Buddha: A Translation of the Majjhima Nikāya*, edited by Bhikkhu Bodhi. Somerville: Wisdom Publications.

Ñāṇananda, Bhikkhu. 2015. *Nibbāna—The Mind Stilled, Volumes No. I–VII, Library Edition*. Mādhya Bhāraya: Pothgulgala Dharmagrantha Dharmasravana.

Nattier, Jan. 1991. *Once Upon a Future Time: Studies in a Buddhist Prophecy of Decline*. Berkeley: Asian Humanities Press.

———— 1992. "The Heart Sūtra: A Chinese Apocryphal Text?" *Journal of the International Association of Buddhist Studies* 15.2: 153–223.

———— 2003. *A Few Good Men: The Bodhisattva Path According to the Inquiry of Ugra (Ugraparipṛcchā)*. Honolulu: University of Hawai'i Press.

———— 2004. "Dīpaṃkara." In *Encyclopedia of Buddhism*, edited by R. E. Buswell, 230. New York: Macmillan Reference.

Norman, K.R. 1984. "The Four Noble Truths: A Problem of Pāli Syntax." In *Indological and Buddhist Studies: Volume in Honour of Professor J.W. de Jong on his Sixtieth Birthday*, edited by L.A. Hercus, 377–91. Delhi: Sri Satguru.

———— 1988. "Pāli Lexicographical Studies V." *Journal of the Pali Text Society* 12: 49–63.

Oldenberg, Hermann. 1879. *The Dīpavaṃsa: An Ancient Buddhist Historical Record, Edited and Translated.* London: Williams and Norgate.

Olivelle, Patrick. 2004. *The Law Code of Manu: A New Translation Based on the Critical Edition.* Oxford: Oxford University Press.

Pagel, Ulrich 1995. *The Bodhisattvapiṭaka: Its Doctrines, Practices, and Their Position in Mahāyāna Literature.* Tring: The Institute of Buddhist Studies.

Paṇḍita, Sayadaw U. 1992/1993. *In this Very Life: The Liberating Teachings of the Buddha,* translated by U Aggacitta. Kandy: Buddhist Publication Society.

Pāsādika, Bhikkhu. 2015. *The Kāśyapaparivarta.* New Delhi: Aditya Prakashan.

Perreira, Todd LeRoy. 2012. "Whence Theravāda? The Modern Genealogy of an Ancient Term." In *How Theravāda Is Theravāda? Exploring Buddhist Identities,* edited by P. Skilling, J. A. Carine, C. Cicuzza, and S. Pakdeekham, 443–571. Chiang Mai: Silkworm Books.

Rahula, Walpola. 1971. "L'idéal du bodhisattva dans le Theravāda et le Mahāyāna." *Journal Asiatique* 259: 63–70.

Ratnayaka, Shanta. 1985. "The Bodhisattva Ideal of the Theravāda." *Journal of the International Association of Buddhist Studies* 8.2: 85–110.

Salomon, Richard. 2018. *The Buddhist Literature of Ancient Gandhāra: An Introduction with Translations.* Boston: Wisdom Publications.

Samuels, Jeffrey. 1997. "The Bodhisattva Ideal in Theravāda Buddhist Theory and Practice: A Reevaluation of the Bodhisattva-Śrāvaka Opposition." *Philosophy East and West* 47.3: 399–415.

Silk, Jonathan A. 2002. "What, If Anything, Is Mahāyāna Buddhism? Problems of Definitions and Classifications." *Numen* 49: 355–405.

Skilling, Peter. 2003. "Three Types of Bodhisatta in Theravādin Tradition: A Bibliographical Excursion." In *Buddhist and Indian Studies in Honour of Professor Sodo Mori,* 91–102. Hamamatsu: Kokusai Bukkyoto Kyokai.

———— 2013. "Vaidalya, Mahāyāna, and Bodhisatva in India: An Essay towards Historical Understanding." In *The Bodhisattva Ideal: Essays on the Emergence of Mahāyāna,* edited by Bhikkhu Ñāṇatusita, 69–162. Kandy: Buddhist Publication Society.

Snellgrove, David. 1987/2002. *Indo-Tibetan Buddhism: Indian Buddhists and Their Tibetan Successors.* Boston: Shambhala Publications.

Sponberg, Alan. 1992. "Attitudes toward Women and the Feminine in Early Buddhism." In *Buddhism, Sexuality, and Gender*, edited by J. Cabezon, 3–36. Delhi: Sri Satguru.

——— 1997. "Green Buddhism and the Hierarchy of Compassion." In *Buddhist and Ecology: The Interconnection of Dharma and Deeds*, edited by M. E. Tucker and D. R. Williams, 351–76. Cambridge: Harvard University Press.

Tanemura Ryugen. 2009. "Superiority of Vajrayāna Part II: Superiority of the Tantric Practices Taught in the *Vajrayānāntadvayanirākaraṇa (rDo rje theg pa'i mtha' gñis sel ba)." In *Genesis and Development of Tantrism*, edited by S. Einoo, 487–514. University of Tokyo: Institute of Oriental Culture.

Thanissara. 2015. *Time to Stand Up: An Engaged Buddhist Manifesto for Our Earth—The Buddha's Life and Message through Feminine Eyes*. Berkeley: North Atlantic Books.

Ṭhānissaro, Bhikkhu. 2015. "On Ordaining Bhikkhunīs Unilaterally." https://discourse.suttacentral.net/uploads/default/original/2X/8/8b0f275a499d7f5a112eae2f409b4aca2a41f03a.pdf.

——— 2018. "A Trojan Horse: Unilateral Bhikkhunī Ordination Revisited." https://discourse.suttacentral.net/uploads/default/original/3X/a/9/a91044fba474217f7f384cafce27918afed51404.pdf.

Thondup, Tulku. 1989/1996. *The Practice of Dzogchen by Longchen Rabjam*. Ithaca: Snow Lion Publications.

Tilakaratne, Asanga. 2000. "Saṅgīti and Sāmaggī: Communal Recitation and the Unity of the Saṅgha." *Buddhist Studies Review* 17.2: 175–97.

van Schaik, Sam 2004. *Approaching the Great Perfection: Simultaneous and Gradual Approaches to Dzogchen Practice in Jigme Lingpa's Longchen Nyingtig*. Boston: Wisdom Publications.

Verardi, Giovanni. 2018. *The Gods and the Heretics: Crisis and Ruin of Indian Buddhism*. New Delhi: Aditya Prakashan.

Vieten, Cassandra, H. Wahbeh, B. R. Cahn, K. MacLean, M. Estrada, P. Mills, M. Murphy, S. Shapiro, D. Radin, Z. Josipovic, D. E. Presti, M. Sapiro, J. C. Bays, P. Russell, D. Vago, F. Travis, R. Walsh, and A. Delorme. 2018. "Future Directions in Meditation Research: Recommendations for Expanding the Field of Contemplative Science." *PloS one* 13(11): e0205740.

von Hinüber, Oskar. 1987/1994: "Buddhist Law and the Phonetics of Pāli, A Passage from the Samantapāsādikā on Avoiding Mispronunciation in

Kammavācās." In *Selected Papers on Pāli Studies,* edited by O. von Hinüber, 198–232. Oxford: Pali Text Society.

———— 2002. [Review of] "Contemporary Buddhism. An Interdisciplinary Journal." *Indo-Iranian Journal,* 45: 266–69.

von Rospatt, Alexander. 1995. *The Buddhist Doctrine of Momentariness: A Survey of the Origins and Early Phase of this Doctrine up to Vasubandhu.* Stuttgart: Franz Steiner Verlag.

Waldschmidt, Ernst. 1948. *Die Überlieferung vom Lebensende des Buddha: Eine vergleichende Analyse des Mahāparinirvāṇasūtra und seiner Textentsprechungen, zweiter Teil, Vorgangsgruppe V–VI.* Göttingen: Vandenhoeck & Ruprecht.

Walshe, Maurice. 1987. *Thus Have I Heard: The Long Discourses of the Buddha.* London: Wisdom Publications.

Wangchuk, Dorji. 2007. *The Resolve to Become a Buddha: A Study of the Bodhicitta Concept in Indo-Tibetan Buddhism.* Tokyo: International Institute for Buddhist Studies.

Wayman, Alex. 1977. *Yoga of the Guhyasamājatantra: The Arcane Lore of Forty Verses—A Buddhist Tantra Commentary.* Delhi: Motilal Banarsidass.

Yamabe Nobuyoshi, and F. Sueki. 2009. *The Sutra on the Concentration of Sitting Meditation (Taishō Volume 15, Number 614) Translated from the Chinese of Kumārajīva.* Berkeley: Numata Center for Buddhist Translation and Research.

Young, R. F., and G. P. V. Somaratna. 1996. *Vain Debates: The Buddhist-Christian Controversies of Nineteenth-Century Ceylon.* Vienna: Institut für Indologie der Universität Wien.

Image Credits

Index

About the Author

BHIKKHU ANĀLAYO is a scholar of early Buddhism and a meditation teacher.

What to Read Next from Wisdom Publications

Rebirth in Early Buddhism and Current Research
Bhikkhu Anālayo

"Bhikkhu Anālayo offers a detailed study of the much-debated Buddhist doctrine of rebirth and a survey of relevant evidence. He also investigates the Pāli chantings of Dhammaruwan, who at a very young age would spontaneously chant ancient and complex Buddhist suttas. I first met Dhammaruwan when he was seven years old, when my teacher, Anagarika Munindraji, and I visited him and his family in Sri Lanka. *Rebirth in Early Buddhism and Current Research* illuminates a complex topic with great clarity and understanding." —Joseph Goldstein, author of *Mindfulness: A Practical Guide to Awakening*

In the Buddha's Words
An Anthology of Discourses from the Pali Canon
Bhikkhu Bodhi

"It will rapidly become the sourcebook of choice for both neophyte and serious students alike." —*Buddhadharma*

What's Wrong with Mindfulness (and What Isn't)
Zen Perspectives
Edited by Robert Meikyo Rosenbaum and Barry Magid

"This book is the best thing I've read on mindfulness and the mindfulness movement." —David Loy, author of *A New Buddhist Path*

Women Practicing Buddhism
American Experiences
Edited by Peter N. Gregory and Susanne Mrozik

"Fascinating." —Susan Piver

Hidden Lamp
Stories from Twenty-Five Centuries of Awakened Women
Edited by Zenshin Florence Caplow and Reigetsu Susan Moon

"An amazing collection. This book gives the wonderful feel of the sincerity, the great range, and the nobility of the spiritual work that women are doing and have been doing, unacknowledged, for a very long time. An essential and delightful book." —John Tarrant, author of *The Light Inside the Dark: Zen, Soul, and the Spiritual Life*

About Wisdom Publications

Wisdom Publications is the leading publisher of classic and contemporary Buddhist books and practical works on mindfulness. To learn more about us or to explore our other books, please visit our website at wisdomexperience.org or contact us at the address below.

Wisdom Publications
199 Elm Street
Somerville, MA 02144 USA

We are a 501(c)(3) organization, and donations in support of our mission are tax deductible.

Wisdom Publications is affiliated with the Foundation for the Preservation of the Mahayana Tradition (FPMT).